Betsy Ross and the Flag

BETSY ROSS

AND

THE FLAG

★

by JANE MAYER

Illustrated by GRACE PAULL

RANDOM HOUSE · NEW YORK

Contents

PART ONE

What Is a Flag?   vii

1. Betsy Wonders   3
2. Mr. Griscom's Answer   13
3. The Stamp Act   22
4. No Longer a Quaker   30
5. The Quilting Bee   38

PART TWO

6. A Rallying Sign   53
7. The Grand Union Flag   64
8. John Ross, Patriot   71
9. Washington Returns to Philadelphia   78
10. Difficulties and Confusions   86
11. The Flag Committee   94
12. The Visit   104
13. Betsy Makes a Flag   113

PART THREE

14. Afternoon in Congress   127
15. The Makeshift Flag   139
16. The Star Spangled Banner   150
17. How Many Stars and Stripes?   159
When It Happened   170

What Is a Flag?

WHAT DOES IT TAKE TO MAKE A FLAG? CLOTH? A
design? Color? Cutting? Sewing? Everyone knows
that it takes all these. But we do not always stop to
think that it takes something else besides. A flag
must be an idea, it must be a symbol. The symbol
and idea have a feeling and give a feeling.

When people first learn and know about their

own flag, they discover that the feeling the flag gives is one of belonging. "We belong to it and it belongs to us," they say. And because people like to belong, like to belong to their families and to their schools, to their teams and to their clubs, they like also to belong to a country.

But belonging to a country after a while means preferring that country, learning what it is like and choosing to stay there. It means swearing allegiance to the flag of that country, really belonging to that flag.

We, in the United States, want to belong to our country and so to the Stars and Stripes because of an idea on which the government of the United States is built. This basic idea is that there is nothing in the world so important as a human being and that every human being has a right to "life, liberty and the pursuit of happiness." We, unlike many other nations, recognize that the purpose of the government in the United States is to serve the individual and give him his chance to have life, liberty and the pursuit of happiness. We rejoice that its purpose is to make the human being free. Yet we insist its purpose is also to develop a sense of responsibility in a citizen so that his own freedom can not go far enough to let him take away life, liberty and the pursuit of happiness from any of his fellow beings.

We, in the United States, want to belong to our country because each and every citizen in it has a chance to say how he wants his government to be run. We want to feel that we can vote for laws and for officials, and that those laws and officials will be the ones the majority of the voters choose. We want to be free to think and to judge and to choose. We want to be able to accept what most of the people vote to have.

After some study of our history, we know that we want to belong to our own particular country because strong men and women made it come alive, and strong men and women have kept it alive. Sometimes their strength was in fighting.

Sometimes it was in not fighting. Sometimes it was in having ideals and principles and sticking to those. Sometimes their strength was just having the courage to know they were right, or having the courage to admit they were wrong.

We want to belong to the United States and to the Stars and Stripes because we like it here. We like the trees and the sky and the grass. We like the cities. We like the buildings. We like the oceans, lakes and rivers. We like the fishing and the hunting, the wild animals and our domestic pets. We like the automobiles, and the movies, radios and television; the funny papers and ball games; the books and libraries. We like the people, the ones who talk like us and the ones who talk differently, the ones who look like us and the ones who are different.

We know perfectly well that not every one of us likes all these things. But we are aware that all of us like enough of these things to feel comfortable here in our own country and to feel we would like to stay here.

We want to belong because it is a country that believes in helping other people, welcoming the newcomer to our shores and trying to assist people in other countries.

Our country appeals to us because it is still young and strong and growing. It needs us. It believes that all countries can, some day, find a peaceful way of working together. It does not know exactly how this can be done. It has made mistakes and it needs us to help correct those mistakes. It gives much to us and expects much from us.

We see our flag high on a flagpole, with its strong, clean colors fluttering bright against the sky. It is beautiful. It is familiar. When we see it we do not think of all the things the flag means and stands for. But we feel them. They are part of us. And so our flag is part of us, too.

Then we would like to find out when this flag that is part of us was first made, why it was made, who made it, who used it and how they used it.

Most people in the United States say that it was Betsy Ross who made the first Stars and Stripes. Some say she did not. But everyone agrees that no matter who made it, the valuable thing is that that flag *was* made, and that we still use the same kind of flag and that we expect to keep our flag and to work for it.

So it does not matter, too much, that some people say Betsy Ross did not make the first Stars and Stripes. These same people who say she did not, admit all the other facts of her life. They know Betsy Griscom Ross did make flags. They know who her parents were and what they stood for. They know how she felt about our country. They know of no other woman or man who can be proved to have made the first flag or of any other person who even claims to have made it.

If we go along with the ones who doubt the

Betsy Ross story, we say maybe she did not make the first American flag. But if we look around a little farther we can also say, maybe she did make it. She could have. And so we keep the tale of Betsy Ross and her first flag as a halfway legend. We like the story even when we are not quite sure. What we are sure about is that whether Betsy Ross was important or not, the flag itself is more important than she was. It is more important because it stands not for just one person but for all of us.

JANE MAYER

PART ONE

1

Betsy Wonders

BETSY GRISCOM WAS DISCOURAGED. SHE WAS twelve years old, and growing up very fast. She would soon be a woman. And she could think of nothing she would ever be able to do when she became a woman which some older, wiser person had not already done before her.

It was a fine spring morning in Philadelphia in the year 1764. But Betsy was too busy thinking even to notice that spring was in the air, and as she walked the few blocks from her home to her school, she dragged along behind one of her younger sisters. Her blue eyes looked down sadly at the brick sidewalk. Her head was bent so low that the wide Quaker bonnet, concealing enough at any time, entirely hid her face.

Finally her sister turned around. "Come along, Betsy," she said. "Thee'll be late."

"It's only seven thirty," Betsy said. "There's half an hour till school time." Then she raised her head and the eyes, so quick to change, were bright and eager. "Let's go down to the river for just a little look."

Her sister said "No" at first. Then urged by Betsy, she finally said "Yes."

They went downhill, crossing a narrow cobble-

4

stoned street and then another, until they were at the foot of High Street.

Here they could see the Delaware River, sparkling in the early sunlight and filled with sailing ships from foreign countries. The girls were familiar with this part of the river but they knew that the Delaware also flowed on, ninety miles to the sea, and that the river was a broad deep highway all the way. They themselves had never gone as far away as ninety miles and they might never go that far, but every day in their home and at school they made use of many things brought to them by the ocean-going vessels. And almost every day they heard how the people of Pennsylvania were making for themselves more and more of the articles they needed, because they were growing more and more annoyed with the large duty they had to pay on goods they imported from England.

Here on the river some of the ships were at anchor with their sails folded. Others were arriving or leaving and so they had at least part of the sails up and their flags flying. The flags on ships from England were blue with interlocking crosses, the white X-shaped cross of St. Andrew and the red cross of St. George. These flags were the Union Jack and proclaimed English nationality. They flapped in the breeze, and made a little whipping sound.

"The flags are pretty," Betsy's sister said.

Betsy looked at these banners. Then she said, "A flag could be prettier than that."

After a little the sister had seen enough and she started to turn back toward school.

"Wait just a little," Betsy begged. "We have time enough to see the ferryboat come in."

They stood perfectly still above the river, watching the ferryboat come toward its dock. They could see the churning water behind this big flat barge and they knew that a paddle wheel was turning, turning to make the boat go. They could see the four horses in the center of the barge walk round and round. The girls knew that the walking

"The flags are pretty," Betsy's sister said.

horses turned a cylinder and that the turning of the cylinder made the paddle wheel revolve.

Betsy, born in Philadelphia, and living there always, had seen this river and this ferry constantly. But she never grew tired of them. Now, as the ferry lumbered toward her, her spirit went to meet it. She felt almost as if she was the one who would tie up the boat, welcome the passengers from it and send them on their way to work throughout this humming, thriving town.

Then she remembered her discouragement. She swung her foot back and forth, scuffing the toe of her shoe against a cobblestone. (Her thrifty Quaker parents would feel duty-bound to scold her for the wastefulness of scuffing, but she did not think of this now.) "That's what I mean," she said.

Her sister did not understand what Betsy was talking about, but this was not unusual. There were times when none of Betsy's sisters understood, times when her mother did not, many times when her mother and father were too busy with their large family to try to understand. Betsy knew this, but when she felt like it she thought aloud, anyhow.

"I mean," she said, trying to explain, "this is the year 1764. Everything has already happened. We can only read about it in books or have people tell us stories about it. Like the stories they tell us about our own Philadelphia. This used to be a wilderness right here and brave men came and struggled to make homes. Now it's a city with streets. Some of the streets are even paved with cobbles and they are lighted by tall whale oil lamps and there are three-story brick buildings for people to live and work in. And look at that ferryboat." She was talking fast and excitedly. "No one could improve on that. No one could even think of any better way to make a ferryboat go."

Betsy's sister tugged at her arm. "It is time now for school," she said. "And I'm of no mind to get a flogging."

"I don't want a flogging either," Betsy said. "I'll

race thee there." She lifted her long skirt a few inches above her ankles and started off.

Betsy wore the regular Quaker outfit. She and her sister were dressed like their mother, whose clothes were much like the clothes of all the other Quaker girls and women of Philadelphia. Betsy's dress was long, close-fitting and of a dull gray. Her white muslin kerchief was folded softly about her neck. Her white muslin apron reached nearly to the hem of her skirt. The skirt itself stopped only a little way above the plain, square-toed, buckled shoes, so that only a few inches of her white stockings could be seen.

But as she raced along her skirt flew higher and higher. When the two girls came within sight of the Friends' School, however, they walked quietly and sedately, as they had been taught to do. They went into the schoolhouse, straightening their shoulders and folding their hands primly in front of them. They hung up their bonnets. Then, prim and sedate, they took their places among the other

Quaker children on the rows of hard wooden benches. They took the little sewing bags which they had been carrying on their wrists and placed them on the benches. Then they opened their books and settled down for the long morning of study

2

Mr. Griscom's Answer

FROM EIGHT TO TEN THAT DAY BETSY STUDIED
without much interest. She did not care a great
deal for the reading, the writing and the number
work which came during the first hours of each
morning.

But she did like the later periods, just before

noon, when every student was told to work at the things he did best, the things which he might use in his later life. It was at these times that Betsy sewed, bending close to her work, trying to make it better and better as she went along. This morning she worked on her sampler and the hours passed much faster than they had passed when she was studying.

Betsy approved of the idea of usefulness. She had been brought up that way by her Quaker parents and her Quaker school.

Betsy approved of the idea of beauty, too, although this was something she had learned rather more accidentally. She knew that the sampler on which she had patiently stitched for so many hours was beautiful. She knew that hers was the prettiest sampler in the whole school, that it had the nicest motto and the gayest flowers and the best sewing, and that when finished it would hang in beauty on a wall at home. She knew that there were many different kinds of stitches on it, some difficult to do, but all done well. She knew that the colors of the threads, dyed for her by her mother, were bright and warm. She knew that this beautiful little piece of sewing was useful, too, because it gave her a chance to practice the stitches she would have to use some day on practical things.

But still, she thought, even if it is a good sampler, it's only a sampler. Everyone makes them. Even my design is almost exactly like a design my mother stitched when she was a little girl.

It was just then that the schoolmaster took his watch from his pocket. The watch was round, thick and heavy, and made of a gray metal like pewter. He walked over to the schoolroom window, looked out and up at the tower of the State House. He looked for some time at the State House. It was a beautiful red building built of bricks sent from England. In it the Governor of Pennsylvania and the other officers of the colony did their work. But everything they did was regulated by the laws of England. The schoolmaster thought of this as he compared the time of his watch with the State House clock. But he did not speak to the children about it because they took it for granted that Pennsylvania was governed this way and always would be governed this way. He simply put his watch back into his pocket and told the children that it was twelve o'clock, time for them to go to their homes for their noon dinner.

Betsy's schoolmates were not different from any other children anywhere. When it was noontime they were hungry and eager to be free.

At home Betsy found her mother, Rebecca Griscom, in front of the big open fireplace in the kitchen, watching over the kettles and stirring the stew for the noonday meal.

The walls of the kitchen were plastered and whitewashed. The brick outside the fireplace was whitewashed, too. The fire was bright and the table was set. Mrs. Griscom, in her plain Quaker dress, with her white apron and the close-fitting white Quaker cap, looked as clean and bright as the room.

Betsy asked if she could help with this noontime meal. When she was told that the other children had already done what there was to do and that she should stay out of the way, she took her low, three-legged stool and sat down to wait. The smell of the simple good food filled the kitchen and she became hungrier and hungrier. She wanted to open the door of the oven which was built into the side of the fireplace so that she could find out what was being baked. But she knew that when she was told to stay out of the way, she must obey unquestioningly.

Soon her father, Samuel Griscom, came in. He smiled at his family as he hung up his beaver hat and went to the Welsh dresser to wash his hands.

Betsy's father, like his father and grandfather before him, was a carpenter. He was good at his trade and worked hard. He was also an important

man in Philadelphia, interested in the doings of
the Friends Meeting, interested in Pennsylvania
politics, and in the affairs of the thirteen Colonies.
He did not talk very much, but when he did his
family listened.

The children liked to hear him tell about William Penn, that great, good Quaker who had
founded their Colony of Pennsylvania and their
city of Philadelphia. They liked to hear how the
English government had owed money to Penn and
how, instead of taking the money, Penn had asked
to be repaid in land in the New World. They liked
to hear how Penn had believed that everyone
should worship God exactly as that person pleased.
And they liked to hear, too, how Penn had felt
people could settle their quarrels by talking them
out instead of warring over them, and how he
had bought land from the Indians instead of steal-
ing it from them or fighting them for it. They
liked to hear how settlers had followed Penn and
had tried to live up to his beliefs.

18

The children were not supposed to ask their father to tell them stories nor to ask him to help them straighten out things that were bothering them. They had been taught to wait until he wanted to talk to them. Sometimes, however, Betsy talked to him before he addressed her. But this was only when something quite serious was on her mind. Now, even though she was hungry and she knew he was too, she could not wait. She pounced on him with the thoughts she had had that morning on her way to school.

"Thee sees how it is," she said after a while. "It isn't only the ferryboat that is as good as it can be. Everything is. If people have to travel a long way on land, they do not have to go on horseback or on foot; they can travel faster in a horse-drawn coach. Why, even in this house, everything has already been invented that can be done. We know how to spin and weave and dye. We know how to make candles so we can light our house in the evening. We know how to keep our house warm in winter with paper at the windows, and with great logs in the fireplace. We have a spring house to keep our food fresh." She shook her head sadly. "What is there left for us children to do when we grow up?" she asked.

Betsy's father looked at her and smiled. "It is not necessary to do something new to be useful," he said. "Industry itself is enough, even if the task is an old one. Some day thee will marry and do as thy mother does. Thee will worship God and tend a home and help and love other people."

"And will I be happy?" Betsy wanted to know.

"That will follow," her father said. "But that is not what we Friends seek first." He sat down at the table and when all were quiet, he said a blessing. Then he began to eat. He ate gravely and quietly with his eyes on the pewter plate in front of him.

After a while he looked at Betsy. He smiled again a little, but his tone was serious. "I did not say all I believe about doing new things," he said.

"There is always something new to do. But we do not always see it when it comes. Sometimes we are afraid because it is new and we refuse it. This is not the best way to do. When something new comes our way it is best to think: I have not done this thing before and perhaps no one else has done it before. But it is a good thing to do and I know I can do it if I try."

Betsy stared at her father and listened hard. She felt reassured. She felt that her father had said something which would make her strong. She repeated his words to herself. *I know I can do it if I try.*

Many, many things were to happen to Betsy after that day, but she never forgot the words her father had spoken.

3

The Stamp Act

SOMETHING OF GREAT IMPORTANCE HAPPENED IN the Colonies during the years that Betsy was thirteen and fourteen. She heard a lot of talk about it, but it did not change anything at school or at home, so it did not seem important to her. As far as she could tell, her life was just the same. But actually this happening was the beginning of a changed way of life for her and for all Americans who came after her. It brought about the first open stirring of revolt in the Colonies.

The something that happened was the Stamp Act. This was a law, passed by the Parliament in England, for the American Colonies. The law said that every legal document of every kind in the Colonies had to be written on paper which the English government sold and on which the English government put a stamp. This stamp was, of course, a tax and it cost anywhere from a few pennies up to thirty dollars, depending on what kind of legal document was being written. Newspapers, pamphlets and almanacs also had to be printed on paper with the stamp. Even advertisements were taxed by means of a stamp.

The first time that Betsy paid any attention to this was when she noticed that all the bells in Philadelphia were silent.

'What is the matter?" she asked her mother.

Mrs. Griscom was making candles by pouring tallow into the tube-shaped metal molds. But she stopped for a minute to explain that the Stamp Act meant taxation without representation. The people were getting taxed without being allowed to vote or have representatives vote for them. When she had explained it, she said that the people in all the Colonies were angry about the new law and were taking different ways of showing it. "Here they muffled the bells," she said. "In Boston they tolled them solemnly. In New York thousands of people marched through the streets with big placards against the Stamp Act."

Because Betsy had no legal documents and because she did not understand much about taxation without representation, none of this seemed worth so much fuss. And because no women ever voted then, she did not think about the Stamp Act again for nearly a year. Then she heard that it had been repealed and so was no longer a law.

The rejoicing over the repeal was noisy and full of color. Cannons were fired, speeches were made, bonfires were lighted. Betsy liked the excitement, but she still did not really understand what was responsible for it.

On the day that the Philadelphians heard about the British Parliament's repeal of the Stamp Act, Betsy went out with her father and walked around the city and down toward the river.

Mr. Griscom looked very fine that day. He had on his usual Quaker clothes—his wide-brimmed hat, his dark brown suit with the knee breeches and the long-waisted coat with padded coat skirts. There were deep white cuffs on his sleeves and a stock of finely pleated white linen was at his neck. He was carrying his cane and tapping it pleasantly as he went along, and his eyes darted about looking for people to talk to.

As they were passing one of the coffee houses where men gathered for friendly talk, two acquaintances of Betsy's father came out and joined them.

Mr. Griscom, who followed all the Quaker rules of behavior, did not raise his hat in salute to them. But the others were not Quakers, so they took off their hats and bowed to Betsy. This made her feel like a young woman instead of a girl of fourteen, and because she felt that way she decided she should listen and pay attention to the talk of the men.

She heard them repeating many of the things her mother had told her when the Stamp Act had been a law. But now they were not just saying that they ought to object to this law. They were saying that the Colonies had already objected and had proved to England that they meant what they said. They did not want to be free from England. They only wanted to have a voice in the making of the laws under which they were taxed.

"The rights and grievances of the Colonies are being understood at last," one of the friends of Mr. Griscom said. "We have shown England that even though we belong to her, we will not stand for unjust laws."

"Yes," the other man said. "Our resistance is having an effect."

They had come to the river and stood looking at the familiar sight of water and ships, sailors and docks and cargoes, and at the flags which told at a glance from what country each ship had sailed.

That day, in the river, there happened to be ships from only two places—England and the Colonies—and so there were only two different kinds of flags. The British ships carried the Union Jack—red, white and blue interlocking crosses. The ships of the Colonies flew one called the Union Flag of Great Britain. This was a flag which the English King had decreed should be used on ships from the Overseas Plantations, as he called the Colonies. It was exactly like the Union Jack except that it had a plain white shield in the center.

The older of the two men who had joined them stared at one of the flags from England. "Sometimes in the past year I have looked at that British flag almost with hate," he said. "But now that they have repealed the Stamp Act, I can again respect His Majesty's ensign."

"The flag is only a symbol of the King and the country," Mr. Griscom said. "If the King and the country respect the rights of all of us, then we can respect their flag. Otherwise we cannot."

His friend interrupted him. "I agree with you," the man said. "And I do not trust this King George. There may be grave trouble yet. They will wait awhile and then think of other ways to tax us without asking us or without giving us any voice in the government. We will have to resist that. Then what?"

Betsy's father shook his head. "I do not know what will happen," he said. "I am against all fighting, as thee knows. But I do know that we must find some way to live in freedom and peace."

4

No Longer a Quaker

IN 1773 BETSY GRISCOM BECAME BETSY ROSS. HER
marriage to young John Ross changed her name,
took her out of her parents' home, set her up in a
comfortable brick house of her own, and made her
a partner and a helper in her husband's business.
These were all pleasant things.

But there was one thing that came to Betsy with her marriage which was not pleasant. She could no longer be a Quaker. This was because her husband was not a Quaker, and the Quakers did not approve of marriage to outsiders.

Betsy's parents talked to her about this many times before the marriage took place. And the talks were all very much the same. They did not object to John Ross as a person. In fact, they liked him. But they thought their daughter should marry a man of their own church.

One evening the Griscom family was gathered as usual in the familiar whitewashed kitchen. The candles burned brightly in their pewter holders. The fire in the open fireplace threw a pinkish light over the walls and the sturdy hand-hewn beams. It shone across the red brick floor. Everything looked comfortable; but nothing really was because the people in the room were in the midst of a quiet, steady argument.

Betsy sat erect on a wood-backed chair and embroidered while she listened and talked. Her mother sat at the spinning wheel, pushing the treadle with her foot and skillfully drawing out the finished linen thread. Betsy's sisters were knitting long heavy woolen stockings, for the family needed so many things which had to be made at home that no one could remain idle long. Mr. Griscom was, for once, doing nothing. He sat at the plain wooden table where they usually ate their meals, his elbows resting on the table.

All through the talking, Betsy's mother said little. Although men and women were equal in Quaker church affairs, she was used to having her husband set the rules of the house and discipline the children. On most evenings her face was bright and calm, but tonight she had a stern look. That look told Betsy how her mother felt about this coming marriage. The daughter knew that her mother and father were in agreement and that both disapproved her choice of a husband.

"Thee must not do this thing," Mr. Griscom

said. He spoke with force, as if this were the first time he had said it instead of the twentieth.

"I must, Father." Betsy's voice was very quiet. Her hands continued busily with the embroidery. "John Ross is the man I shall marry. I even believe that God intends him as the husband for me."

"This I do not believe," Samuel Griscom answered. "To marry one outside the Society of Friends is an unequal yoking. Our Book of Discipline states this."

"Yes, Father, I know it says that," Betsy said. "But John is a good man. He is even a religious man." She smiled with a touch of mischief. "An Episcopalian can be religious, too, I think."

"The Episcopalians do not respect the Friends," Betsy's mother said, "nor do they respect the Friends' beliefs." She looked sadly at her daughter. "They have held us up to scorn and ridicule for refusing to fight in wars."

Betsy walked to the fireplace and threw some

wood upon the fire. Then, standing there, she turned to face her mother. "But John would not hold us up to scorn or ridicule," she said. "He is the son of a minister. He understands."

"We Quakers do not even understand ministers," her father said. His face flushed. "We do not believe in an ordained man who is paid to lead a flock. We let those speak out in Meeting who feel ready to speak. We do not set one man apart as a man of God. We believe that we are all alike."

Betsy picked up the small stool she had used as a child and carried it across the room. When she had placed it near her father's feet and had sat on it, looking up at him, she seemed almost like a child again. But her words were grown-up and full of meaning.

"The Friends have taught me to believe that we are all alike," she said. "I remember thee told me that William Penn said to the Indians, 'We are all in one mankind; we are all of one flesh and blood.'

Because I have been taught this it does not seem right to me to hear my father now say, 'Do not marry this man because he is different.' William Penn said, too, that we are all to be allowed to believe what we like."

"Of course all may believe as they like," Samuel Griscom said. "The Friends persecute no people for their beliefs. But that does not mean that we marry with those of another religious persuasion."

Betsy was silent for a while. She thought that her father was old-fashioned and did not understand how a young woman felt. But because she respected many of his ideas, she had given him many chances to explain why he was against her marriage. She had thought he could perhaps convince her she was wrong. Now she knew he could not. She had to speak as she would always speak, strongly for the thing she believed in.

"I am sorry, Father," she said finally. "I do not want to go against my parents. But each of us must do what he thinks is right. And I must marry John."

"Even though thee be read out of the Meeting?" her father asked.

"Even though I be read out of the Meeting," Betsy said. "And I know it will happen. I know that after I marry John Ross, the Quakers will disown me." She looked pleadingly at him, then in the same way at her mother. "But I will not disown the Quakers," she said. "I'll go to John's church, but I'll still have all the things in me the Friends and my parents taught me. Those things do not change."

Samuel Griscom sighed. He had a busy day planned for the next day and much to think about besides this one daughter. He had his own carpentry work to do and some work on Carpenter's Hall besides. Also, he had to go to a meeting of the master builders.

"Very well," he said. "But I shall try again to dissuade thee."

Betsy smiled. "I cannot claim that my stubbornness is a virtue," she said. "I can only claim that it is something I have. I could not be a Griscom without it."

Samuel got up and walked over to a peg on the wall where he had hung his wide-brimmed Quaker hat. He set the hat squarely on his head and started toward the door.

Betsy held her hand out toward him, asking him to wait a moment. "There is one more thing I want to say," she said. "I think it will please all the family. John has worked hard as an apprentice at Webster's Upholstery Shop. I have worked to learn upholstering, too. Some day, soon after we marry, we hope to have a shop of our own. Our work will be the best we can do. And I will make my family proud of me."

5

The Quilting Bee

ABOUT A YEAR AND A HALF AFTER BETSY WAS
married to John Ross, she gave a party. But like
most parties of those days, this one was not just for
sociability, although there was much sociability
in it. This one had another purpose, too. It was a
quilting bee.

For many weeks, in her spare time, Betsy had been sewing together bright scraps of material. These scraps were odds and ends saved from worn-out clothes, leftovers from new dresses and shirts, and remnants from furniture covering. They were of widely assorted sizes and shapes and colors, but she had pieced them together to make an attractive pattern. Then the whole thing had been mounted on a thin layer of wool and that on a bed-size oblong of dark material. It was now ready to be quilted. When the quilting was finished, Betsy would have a warm and gay bed covering which would last for years.

She had invited nine or ten of her women friends to come in to spend the day with her. In her living room she had attached the patchwork to a stretching frame and had laid this frame out on her largest table. Around the table she had then placed her chairs and chairs belonging to one of her neighbors. Although it was June, she lighted a small fire, just to make her room look cozy.

The women who came to the party knew what to expect. They themselves had all given or attended parties like this. They knew that for one woman to quilt a bed cover by herself would be a tedious and lonely job. But they knew also that, working together, they could quilt the whole spread in a day, and that they could talk and gossip and laugh while they worked. So they brought their children who were too young to play alone, and brought their needles and work bags. Then they settled down to a pleasant day.

Betsy was very glad to have them there. She had shined her brass candlesticks and her pewter plates. She had washed her hand-braided rugs. She had polished her furniture with a cloth soaked in beeswax. She was proud of the small two-and-a-half-story brick house on Arch Street where she and John had both their home and their upholstery business, so she liked to see things bright and shining for guests.

Betsy sat working at the table, chatting with her

friends and listening to their chatter. She no longer wore the straight simple clothes and the wide bonnet of the Quakers, for she was no longer a Quaker. Her prediction that she would be disowned by the Society of Friends had come true. She had been sorry at the beginning to offend her parents and her sisters and some of her old friends, but her parents and many of the others had now forgiven her.

And she had discovered that neither the change from the "thee" and "thou" speech nor the change in the type of clothing she wore made a great difference to her. So now she was dressed like most of the other women at the party, in a gown made with a tight bodice, a narrow waist and a full skirt. Hers was blue and had an edging of white around the neck. On her head she wore a cap of thin white material.

As the women worked indoors they could hear many of the sounds from out-of-doors. They heard the children playing *I Spy* or racing games and they heard the barking of dogs. They heard the wagons and carts rumbling over the cobblestoned streets on their way to or from the waterfront. All of these were such ordinary sounds that they made little impression. But suddenly the women heard a new sound.

They stopped talking. They looked up from their work. They looked at one another.

"Horses," someone said.

"But not carts," another said.

"And not coaches."

"Soldiers."

"The Philadelphia Light Horse Troop."

"Of course."

Betsy pushed away from the table and stood up. "Oh, I know what it is." Her voice rose with excitement. Her blue eyes shone. "Don't you remember? This is the day that General Washington is to go to Cambridge to take command of the army. The Philadelphia Light Horse Troop is escorting him."

The guests all dropped their sewing things on the table. They scrambled out of their chairs and rushed to the front door of the house. There they almost collided with some of their children, who were running in to tell them that Washington and the Light Horse Troop were about to pass the house.

As the women ranged themselves along the brick sidewalk, Betsy stood behind them in the doorway, stretching up on tiptoe to see above them.

There were not quite thirty men in the troop, but they and their uniforms and their horses looked bright and dashing. Their Philadelphia Light Horse flag was splendid to see.

It was a flag of yellow silk. In the upper left-hand corner was a canton or field of thirteen stripes—seven blue ones and six silver-white ones. In the center of the yellow flag was an elaborate design with a horse's head and a shield bearing thirteen ribbon ends. On one side of the shield was a kind of angel blowing a trumpet, and on the

43

other an Indian with a great feathered headdress.

General Washington, astride a fine horse, rode with his escort, looking as bright and dashing as the Troop and its Light Horse flag. His uniform was of the colors of the Virginia militia, a blue coat and buff breeches; but he was now commander-in-chief of the Continental armies.

George Washington had received this appointment only six days earlier. The second Continental Congress, meeting in the State House in Philadelphia, had decided that instead of a separate army for each colony, the Colonies needed an army which could protect all of them. The Congress had also decided that the army needed a leader who could think and act. So all the delegates had voted for Washington.

Washington had arrived at the Continental Congress as the delegate from Virginia. He was there as a civilian, but throughout the meetings he had been the only delegate wearing a military uniform. He had not had to tell the Congress what this costume meant. The other delegates knew it was his way of saying that freedom must be fought for. However, even though he believed this, he had not wanted to be the one to command the army. He did not think he was a great enough man for the job. He thought of himself as a forty-three-year-old Virginia planter who would help other people fight for freedom, but who was not intended to be the one to lead them in the fight.

Betsy Ross, seeing him now, with his strong ruddy face and his tall body, thought of what Washington had done a few days before when the Congress first tried to make him take the office of commander-in-chief. At first he refused to do it. But when the Congress told him how badly he was needed, he said he would do it. *He is acting in the way my father described long ago,* Betsy thought. *There is something new for Washington to do. He does not know if he can do it, but he'll try.*

Then Betsy suddenly thought of something else

about him. She remembered the shirts he had ordered from her and for which she had embroidered fine cuffs and ruffles. She had worked hard on this embroidery and she had been very proud of it when it was finished. Now she wondered if she could see those ruffles. She craned her neck and stretched up further on her toes. She could see that he wore a white shirt and that it had long cuffs and a flowing neckpiece. But she could not tell from such a distance whether or not this was her handiwork. She sighed in disappointment.

The little parade passed on. The women waved a last time and then turned back into the Ross home.

Now as they sat down around their quilting, they no longer talked of cooking and making clothes for their families or of how to bring up their children. They talked instead of the exciting and sometimes frightening things that were going on in the Colonies.

46

"George Washington is beginning to believe we should be separated from England," one of the older women said.

"Yes, he is saying that nowadays," a young one answered. "But he said the opposite a year ago. Now he believes that the rights of Englishmen in America have been attacked and that we must fight to defend those rights."

"Colonel Washington . . ." The woman who had said this stopped and laughed. "I guess he's General Washington now. At any rate, he refused to take any pay for being commander. He told the Congress he didn't want money because 'no pecuniary consideration could have tempted me to accept this arduous employment at the expense of my domestic ease and happiness.' "

Betsy sighed. "It's two and a half years since the Boston Tea Party," she said. "That's a long time for things to stay so stirred up."

A friend of Betsy's looked across the quilting

frame at her. "Those men who took the tea chests off the ship and emptied them into the bay . . . What did they call them . . . Mohawks?"

"Yes," Betsy said. "Don't you remember? That was the name for all the anti-tax citizens. The Indian on the Light Horse Flag we just saw is supposed to be a Mohawk. John told me to look closely at that Indian. He represents one of our men in disguise. Why, he has a Continental officer's gold crescent hung around his neck."

"But they needed no disguise at Lexington and at Concord," someone said proudly.

The women stopped working and sat silent. The Battles of Concord and Lexington had taken place just two months before. These battles were so close to them in time and so bound up with what might happen next to them and their families that they were sad and afraid. Indeed they were almost ashamed that they had forgotten the battles for even a little while. They were ashamed that they were sitting here in their usual way, sewing and gossiping. But they knew also that they had to keep on with their useful work and that it was a good thing for them to enjoy themselves when they could.

After a long time Betsy asked, "Do you think it was necessary for those Massachusetts Minute Men to fight the British Regulars? Could the Colonies perhaps have petitioned for rights again?"

All the women began to talk at once.

"Don't you know how many times we have petitioned and been refused?"

"My husband says we must all stand with the people of Massachusetts."

"Mine says the King has repeated the same injuries so often that he has proved he is against us."

"England sent troops to the Colonies in peacetime without asking our permission."

"And England let her soldiers try to arrest John Hancock and Samuel Adams just because they were our leaders and weren't afraid to speak out."

"And the British tried to take our munitions, too."

"But that silversmith, Paul Revere, warned our men in time." *

Soon there were so many voices that no one could hear anything. Finally there was quiet. Then Betsy said the thing that all of them were thinking. "If the fighting must continue, I pray that General Washington and our army will succeed. And to make them succeed, we must all help in every way we can."

* You can read more about Paul Revere in another Landmark Book, *Paul Revere and the Minute Men* by Dorothy Canfield Fisher.

PART TWO

6

A Rallying Sign

GENERAL WASHINGTON, AS HE RODE ON TOWARD
Massachusetts, also was thinking that all the people
in the Colonies must now help in every way they
could. The colonial troops he was going to com-

mand were waiting for him at Cambridge. But the city of Boston was held by the British Regulars. Washington planned to besiege Boston to try to get the British out. It would not be an easy task, nor a quick one, nor a single-handed one.

On the way to Cambridge, Washington and his escort met a messenger riding in the opposite direction. The messenger was hot and sweaty. When he spoke, he spoke very fast, as if he did not have time to catch his breath. Even the horse he rode looked tired and hot.

The messenger told Washington that he was rushing to Philadelphia to tell Congress of the Battle of Bunker Hill.

This was the first direct word Washington had had of the battle, so he asked many questions. The messenger answered them and told how bravely and how well the colonists had fought, even though lack of ammunition had forced them to lose in the end. When Washington heard of the bravery, he was encouraged. Yet, because of the defeat, he was more eager than ever to get to Cambridge. He urged the men on.

The journey was a slow one on horseback and it seemed even slower to the General because he knew of the many problems awaiting him and how serious all these problems were. He would have to take raw, untrained troops and turn them into skilled fighting men. He would have to see that the Congress supplied them with plenty of muskets and gunpowder. It would be his job to persuade Congress to have them well clothed and provided with good nourishing food. He would have to make sure that Congress and the Colonies stood behind him in everything he asked for and did.

But most important of all he knew that he himself would have to give these men from scattered towns and different parts of the country a feeling that they were all in the fight together. He would have to give each man a feeling of belonging to the others and with the others. He had thought about this often, wondering and worrying how he could give them this feeling. He believed he had found an answer to his problem.

Washington believed that these men needed a symbol of belonging. They needed something that would tell them at a glance that they were all together for the same purpose. He believed that these men needed a flag.

They already had some flags. But these flags separated them because each flag represented some little group, or some event or some colony. For instance, there was the Bedford flag of the militia company of Bedford. This had been carried at Concord when the British Regulars were met by the Minute Men and driven off. It was a noble-looking flag and one to be honored because it was the first flag of the American Revolution to go forward under fire and on to victory. It was a victorious-looking flag, too—square and red, with a man's hand in armor on it in silver and gold, and the motto in Latin, "Conquer or Die."

Another flag these men had was the Bunker Hill

flag, the flag of the brave men who at Bunker Hill had twice driven back the British before they themselves ran out of ammunition. The Bunker Hill flag, honored as the first to be borne in a pitched battle of the Revolution, was blue with a white canton. There was a red cross in the canton and a green pine tree in one corner of the cross.

Then there was the flag of Rhode Island with the word *Hope* written in blue above a blue anchor and with white stars in a blue field. There was the flag of the New York Regiment—dark blue silk with a blue fringe—a huge square with the arms of the state on it. And there was another New York flag with a beaver, for industry, as its symbol.

Washington knew that flags like these and others which his men carried were good emblems for small groups. But they were not good for his purpose, because they did not represent his whole army. There was no flag which said, "Here are thirteen colonies all fighting together to defend themselves and each other." No flag said, "Thirteen colonies working together are stronger than thirteen colonies working separately."

He pondered the matter many times as he journeyed toward his command.

Finally on a clear fine morning in July, General Washington, astride his big horse, took command at Cambridge. The troops, on foot, lined up on Cambridge Common before him.

The men looked as he had thought they would. They had no uniforms. Many of them wore their own everyday clothes. A few had the uniforms of the militia of the colony from which they came. They did not have enough guns or the right kinds of guns. They were brave and willing men, but they were untrained and they were not too sure why they were there. It was easy to see that they did not feel they belonged together.

George Washington himself was young for the task that had been given him. He was untrained for it and he was inexperienced, because all the fighting he had done before this had been wilderness fighting. And that was altogether different from the kind of warfare expected of him now.

Washington did not waste much time looking at this army. Instead, he wheeled his horse under an elm tree, faced the troops on the common, held his sword aloft and took command.

A little ripple went over the troops. The men held themselves straighter to match Washington's straightness. They felt taller as if to match his tallness. They felt energetic with his energy. They were brave with his courage. They could almost believe that they too wore the well-fitting long coat and the tight breeches of his blue-and-buff uniform.

Feelings, such as these men had, go back and forth from leader to men and from men to leader. Washington could tell what was happening to his troops and he was glad. He wanted them to feel confidence in him and to be willing to follow him. But he knew this was not enough. He knew that the personality of a leader can count for much, but that it is the cause for which the leader stands that is most important. He wanted the men to feel the cause.

He had said that he was willing to command these troops because the Colonies and their people were drawing together out of a need for common defense. Now the men must begin to feel their unity. Now was the time to show these men a rallying sign.

The rallying sign was ready. It was his newly created flag, the General's flag, the flag which would mark his headquarters as commander-in-chief. Washington had it unfurled.

The flag of the commander-in-chief was plain but striking. It had a blue field, entirely blue. And on this field were thirteen six-pointed white stars.

The men cheered when they saw their commander's flag.

Washington's ruddy face glowed with pleasure. He was glad that this flag had been ready for the men. But still, he thought, looking at the soldiers

The flag of the commander-in-chief was plain but striking.

again, it is not enough. This flag is only a commander's flag. It is too much mine. It should be theirs. It should belong to all of us. We must have another flag, he thought, a flag which means the soldiers and me, and the children and women at home, and the Congress. We must have one which is seen clearly at sea and which is recognized easily on land. We must have a flag which tells us that liberty must be fought for. We must have one which tells us that together we battle and work for liberty.

Washington returned to his headquarters. His blue flag had been hoisted there. He looked at it.

One of his aides spoke to him. "Your new standard is very fine, General," the aide said.

"Yes," Washington said. "But these men need a more striking flag than this. They need one which means union and strength. They are going to have to face hunger and danger and discouragement. A flag will be a sign to them that the suffering is for a reason. I must ask the Congress to provide a Colonial flag."

7

The Grand Union Flag

DURING THE SUMMER, AUTUMN, AND EARLY WIN-
ter of 1775, George Washington knew he had
been right about his soldiers. They were good
men, strong and brave. But they had no feeling
that each and every one of them was important to
the army. They had no feeling at all that they be-

longed together and must stick together. And so, for a long time after Lexington and Bunker Hill, the Colonial army accomplished almost nothing.

Men would disappear from the army without a word. When the General asked, "Where is so and so?" or "Where are the men from such and such a place?" he would receive honest but strange answers. "Oh," he would be told, "he's gone home to work on his farm"; or "They've returned to their homes to harvest the crops"; or "His business wasn't doing well without him so he went back to his shop"; or "His wife was sick and he went home to see her."

Washington did not blame these men for their desertions. He blamed the lack of organization that made them desert. He would look at the remaining troops and when he saw the clothing that was too heavy for them in the summer and too light in the winter, he would wonder why even these men stayed. He would walk around among the troops while they were eating, and when he saw that the food was not good and that there was not nearly enough of it, he would wonder the same thing. When he saw the many banners of the small groups, he would think again, there must be one flag which stands for all of us.

Washington decided he must organize a new army. That is, he must take the old army, add new men to it and urge the deserters to come back. He must keep after Congress for food and supplies and clothing. He must explain over and over again that the present rulers of England did not listen to reason and would only listen to force. He must get a flag for the new army that would be a truer "rallying sign."

Finally Congress and the people began to listen to Washington and to understand what he meant. His strength of character, his energy and activity, his common sense, his ability to organize, all had their effect. As the year 1775 came to an end, the regiments began to fill with new volunteers and with the return of many of the old ones. There

"Oh, he's gone home to work on his farm."

was a strong wave of patriotism. There was hope in the air. Congress saw to it that provisions were supplied. A committee in Congress recommended that the Colonial army have a flag. It was to be called the Grand Union flag. Later on, it was called the Cambridge flag.

On the second of January, 1776, Washington again reviewed the troops on Cambridge Common. They looked better than they had in July, but not a great deal better. Washington knew that the struggle to make an army and to bring this army to victory would still be a long and tiring one. The first step in the struggle was to display the new flag.

The men stood waiting, facing their General. The colorbearers approached. A drum rolled, and the flag was unfurled. The men watched it rise, catch the breeze and flutter. They began to cheer —loud, happy cheers.

Washington looked at the new Grand Union flag. This flag had thirteen horizontal stripes of red and white. In the upper left hand corner, next to the staff, was the old British flag, the Union Jack, with the interlocked red-and-white crosses of St. Andrew and St. George. This flag said, "Thirteen American Colonies *and* England."

George Washington watched the flag and watched the men. This is a better flag, he thought. In those stripes the men can see that all the Colonies belong together. Then he shook his head in disappointment. The field of the flag is not right, he thought. When the men look at that they will feel that they are fighting *for* England. They must feel that they are fighting *against* England. They must know they are fighting *for the Colonies*. This flag will do for the time being. But in the end we must have a flag that is American.

He dismissed the troops and returned slowly to his headquarters.

8

John Ross, Patriot

IF BETSY ROSS HAD NOT BEEN "DISOWNED" YEARS
before by the Quakers because of her marriage, she
might have been disowned now for her feeling
about the war. For certainly if Betsy had been a
man she would have joined the army and been
ready to fight against the British.

This war was not yet spoken of as the Revolution. There had been no Declaration of Independence. But many people felt there should be a declaration, and Betsy was one of these. Other people felt just as strongly that, although the Colonies could demand their rights, they must remain loyal to England. They felt that, if necessary, they must fight on England's side against the Colonies.

In England at this time there was just as much disagreement. The background of many of the colonists and the English was, after all, the same. So there were great numbers of liberty-loving English who felt the Colonies were being mistreated. There were many who felt that loyalty came first. There were also many who did not know the facts at all, because the Colonies were so far away and communication was so poor.

In this argument, the Quakers in America would not side with either the Colonies or England because Quakers did not believe in war. If a young Quaker joined either side to fight—and many of them did join on both sides—he was going against the Friends' beliefs and therefore might be "read out of the Meeting."

Philadelphia was then the second largest English-speaking city in the world. It was also the place where Congress met, the center of much of the news and much of the activity. So it was natural that people in Philadelphia should feel strongly for and against what was going on. Betsy believed herself lucky that she and her husband agreed about these things.

A short time after Washington was made commander-in-chief of the Colonial Army, John Ross decided he would join the Pennsylvania militia. John and Betsy did not have to discuss this very much.

"I am joining," he told her one evening. "I believe I am needed."

For a minute Betsy was too sad to look at him. She closed her eyes and thought of how very much John meant to her and of the hardships and dangers he would encounter. Then she opened her eyes again and said quietly, "I believe it, too, John. You *are* needed."

She walked across the room to her husband and put her arms around him. While she stood there with him she thought, John is now another one who has some new task he must try very hard to do. Then she sat down in a chair and began to look through the things in her mending basket.

"We must see that your clothes are all mended and in order," she said, trying to be very business-like and to cover her feelings. "Perhaps I should knit you some new stockings or a new warm scarf."

John Ross laughed. He knew that with a wife like Betsy there would be no scurry to mend or darn. His clothes were ready that evening, just as they were always ready. But he also knew that when people were sad or frightened, as Betsy must be now, they felt better when they could do something. So he said, "Yes, Betsy. Nights can be cold for a soldier. There are many warm things I shall need."

"I wonder what work they will give you to do," Betsy said.

"Some of the Pennsylvania militiamen have been set to guard the docks here in Philadelphia," John said.

"Oh? Why?"

"Because military supplies are unloaded on these docks and placed in the warehouses here," John Ross said. "Arms and ammunition like that are very hard to come by and are very valuable. They must be guarded night and day."

"Where do the supplies come from?" Betsy said.

"I do not know exactly," John said. "Some say they come from the West Indies. No one is supposed to talk about it much. I do know, though, that there is a committee in Congress which makes secret plans to get the ammunition and bring it here. Our friend Mr. Robert Morris is the president of the committee."

75

"I saw him last Sunday at church," Betsy said. "Usually as we walk out of the door of Christ Church, he speaks to me, but this time he was too busy talking to John Hancock."

"I suppose," John said, "there is so much for the Congress to do nowadays that the delegates must discuss things even on Sundays." He looked at his wife. "I am really glad, Betsy," he said, "that I have decided to do what I can to help out."

Six months later Betsy had reason to remember these words of her young husband. John had been assigned to guard the supplies and ammunition on the wharf. He had gone there at night. There was an explosion of gunpowder. No one knew how the explosion had happened, nor what had caused it. John was killed. He had had his chance to do what he could for the Revolution. He was buried in Christ Church Burying Ground with other pa-triots.

Betsy was greatly saddened, but she had so much

to do that she could not spend time feeling sorry for herself. Now she had to carry on the work of the shop and the work for her country alone.

9

Washington Returns to Philadelphia

THREE MEN OPENED THE TALL WHITE DOOR OF the State House and came out through the wide doorway onto the stoop. They stood still for a minute, then lifted their faces to the pale May sunshine and breathed deeply. Their breathing was that of men who have been thinking and working hard indoors, and who are relieved to be out and away from it for a little while.

The three were General Washington, Robert Morris and George Ross—the latter an uncle of the man Betsy Griscom married—and they had just left a busy session of the Congress. They made a pleasant picture standing together on that white stone stoop, with the fine squared outline of the State House for their background.

Washington, as usual, wore his uniform. His wig was snowy white, and the bow at the back of it was neat and exact. His cocked hat, with the stiff flaps turned up to the crown, was well-blocked and brushed. He was wearing a fine shirt with embroidered cuffs. He looked like what he was, a polished aristocrat from Virginia.

George Ross, who was a lawyer and a Pennsylvania delegate to the Congress, and one who helped supply cannon for colonial defense, was dressed like a businessman. His tight breeches and long coat were plain and gray. But he had fancy buttons on his waistcoat, hand-knit white hose of silk, silver shoe buckles and a white powdered wig.

Robert Morris wore a brown suit with cloth-covered buttons. His plain white shirt had gold sleeve-buttons with his initials on them. Under his double chin was a severe white collar and a jabot. His white wig was worn untied in back. His hat was tilted a little toward his dark brown eyebrows and dark kind eyes.

Washington started down the steps toward the street, but Robert Morris put out a hand to stop him.

"I am glad for your sake, General," Robert Morris said, "that your report to the Congress is finished. It is a great deal to ask of a man that he lead the entire army. But we also brought you back to the capital to give advice on how the war should be continued."

"And I am glad the Congress asked me to come," Washington said. "Even though we have finally driven the British out of Boston, there are still many other threatened points. General Howe is a dangerous opponent. The more Congress understands of the problems, the better. The more Congress can advise me, the better. There is so much disagreement now as to what course we should take. I like to see many people consulting about it."

"But it uses up so much of your time," Robert Morris said.

George Ross looked up admiringly at the tall General with the square determined jaw and chin. "Yes," he said, "but Washington is a man who always manages to make time for everything." He touched the General's sleeve. "Your uniform looks new, sir. Have you had time to attend to that, too?"

The tight line of Washington's lips relaxed and he smiled. "It is not new," he said, "but I am not ashamed to admit that I always have time for clothes. I have not written of late to my London agents, but I used always to do it, to tell them exactly how I wished my pockets to be made or how they should make the piping on the waistcoat."

("And you used to write them, too, about exactly what tableware and ornaments you wanted shipped," Robert Morris said.

"I imagine it was worth the trouble," George Ross said. "I hear the things in your home are beautiful."

"I've always liked good things," Washington said. "I suppose that is one of the reasons I keep demanding the right equipment for our army."

Robert Morris laughed. "And why you keep getting it," he said.

Washington and Morris were great friends. They both knew the General was getting many of the supplies he needed for his army, but they also were well aware that he was not getting nearly enough.

Robert Morris, who had been born in England and now lived in Philadelphia, was a shipping merchant. His ships carried manufactured goods

82

from England to the Colonies and also carried goods from the Colonies to other countries. In the days when the people had been strongly against the Stamp Act, he had refused to let his ships bring imports from Britain. This had meant a loss of money to him, but he was a man of firm principles and strong ideas.

Washington liked the honesty and understanding and warm nature of Robert Morris. He was glad that his friend was a delegate to the Congress and that he was one of the leading representatives of the patriots' cause. He was glad that this popular friend of his was in charge of buying supplies for the army and that he did banking business for the Congress. Washington knew that without Morris, everything would be even more difficult than it now was.

With the wisdom, courage and resolution which Robert Morris had, miracles could be accomplished. So Washington did not mind that Morris teased him about getting things for the army.

In reply to this Washington said, "At least my visit to Philadelphia has done one thing. Everyone in the Congress now knows the dangers if these delays continue." He walked down the steps and the two other men followed him. They went down Walnut Street in the direction of the City Tavern, where Washington was staying with Mrs. Washington. "I wish, though, that I could persuade them of the importance of some of the smaller things."

"What, for instance?" George Ross asked.

"A flag."

The three men had come to a corner. They stopped and stood perfectly still. Ross and Morris looked at Washington. They saw that his ruddy face was flushed and that his high forehead was wrinkled with distress.

"Yes. A flag," Washington said. "We do not even have proper regimental flags. I have asked for them repeatedly. I have just written General Putnam again, asking him to give positive orders to all the colonels to have colors immediately completed for their respective regiments. The men do not know with whom they are fighting, nor for what they are fighting."

"What about the Grand Union flag?" George Ross asked.

"That!" Washington exploded. "Do you know what happened at the siege of Boston? We hoisted that flag above the earthworks and we saluted it with thirteen guns. It was a sign of victory. But our own men did not know it meant victory. When they saw those British crosses in the canton, they took it as a token of submission."

"This is a serious matter," Robert Morris said. "Let us go back to the State House where we can sit down and talk about it."

10

Difficulties and Confusions

WASHINGTON, MORRIS AND GEORGE ROSS WERE ALL
well-known in the town of Philadelphia and the
townspeople were curious about these important
men who were deciding and doing such important
things. So now, as they turned to retrace their

86

steps along the brick sidewalks and through the narrow cobbled streets, people stopped to greet them. Other small groups of people would simply stare at them as they passed. Some of the children who did not know General Washington would wave to him, and he would return their greeting, gravely and politely. Then the children would run indoors to tell their mothers what had happened.

When the three reached the State House once more, they entered the building. In one of the second-story rooms they found a quiet corner and sat down.

"The flag situation is just as bad at sea," Robert Morris said. "In fact, it is almost worse. Because if there is one thing required of a flag, it is that it be easily recognized on a vessel. Our colonial ships are not recognized because we have so many different flags that no one knows for sure to whom the ships belong."

He went on then and gave them a long account of the difficulties of ships and their flags. Wash-

87

ington already knew much of what he told and George Ross knew some of it, but neither of them knew it all, so he gave it in detail:

A navy for the Colonies had been started at just about the same time that Washington had re-organized his army and unfurled the Grand Union or Cambridge flag. The flagship of this little fleet was called the *Alfred*. Her captain was Comman-der Esek Hopkins, who was also commander of the new navy. John Paul Jones was the senior lieuten-ant of the *Alfred* and it had been his duty and his pride to hoist the flag at the stern of his ship, where the national flag flies. This flag, a duplicate of the Grand Union flag—thirteen red-and-white stripes and a canton with the crosses of St. George and St. Andrew—had thus been the first American Navy ensign.

The *Alfred*, like most ships, carried three flags. Besides the ensign, there was a smaller flag, the Jack, flown at the prow, and the special flag of that ship, flown from the mainmast.

The Jack on the *Alfred*, the first American Navy Jack, was hoisted for the first time on the same day as the navy ensign. It was a flag with red-and-white stripes and a rattlesnake spread across the flag. The white stripe nearest the bottom bore the motto, "Don't tread on me."

The flag on the mainmast of the *Alfred* was the commodore's flag. It had been presented to Commander Esek Hopkins by Colonel Christopher Gadsden. Robert Morris, when he came to this part of his account, called it the Gadsden flag. It was bright yellow and it also had a rattlesnake, coiled and ready to strike, and the words, "Don't tread on me."

"The rattlesnake is a good emblem for our country," George Ross said. "I know of no other country where they have such snakes. And a rattlesnake never gives up. Just as we will never give up."

"Furthermore," George Washington said, "they say that a rattler does not strike without just cause. That, too, is like our people."

"I believe," Robert Morris said, "that the emblem was chosen because someone said of the rattlesnake, 'She never wounds until she has generously given notice to her enemy, and cautioned him against the danger of treading on her.' But even if that is true," he went on, "that does not make it a good emblem for use at sea. No one can distinguish the rattler at a distance. And certainly no one can read those words. But the present ensign is even more useless. How can one distinguish nationality with it? It is taken from the flag of the East India Company, so our ships are mistaken for those. It also has the British Union Jack in its canton, so friend and enemy alike believe ours to be British ships."

"What about the privateers?" George Ross asked. "They can't use a navy flag, can they?"

The privateers were privately owned trading ships. They had nothing to do with the navy. But they were being used at that time for many special war jobs. They carried supplies and ammunition.

Once in a while they would even get into a fight. It was important that they, too, be easily recognized as American ships.

"The privateers are as badly off as the naval vessels," Morris said. "Many of them still carry the flag of the colony from which they come and hence they seem to belong to no nation. Others now fly the Merchant flag."

The Merchant flag, he explained, contained thirteen stripes, and nothing else. Sometimes the stripes were red and white, sometimes they were any other colors the captains decided on.

"This Merchant flag shows unity," Morris said. "It shows that the ship represents all the Colonies. Another good thing about the Merchant flag is that there is nothing British on it. But it has one great disadvantage."

"What is that?" Washington asked.

"When a ship is in distress it signals for help by turning its flag upside down. The Merchant flag looks exactly the same whether it is flown right side up or upside down. There is no way to signal distress with it."

Washington got up and began to pace around the room. Finally he returned to the two other men and stopped in front of them. He did not look at them, however. He looked over their heads and out the window toward the sea, where colonial ships were sailing.

"We are agreed on the need for a flag," he said. "But we must do more than agree. We must act. There has been no definite resolution in Congress for a new flag, although there has been much talk of such a resolution. I believe I know why the Congress is still unwilling to vote on a flag. It is because not everyone agrees that the Colonies must cease belonging to England. Until such agreement is reached, we cannot consider ourselves a new and separate country and there can be no new and separate flag."

He stepped back a little, dropped his head, and from his great height looked down at them. Something stalwart and rugged about him made both men rise to their feet, as if they would follow where he led.

"The time for the separation from England is not far off," Washington said. "Let me ask you gentlemen something. If a declaration of our wish to separate and our reasons for separating were to be written by the Congress, would you sign it?"

"I would," Robert Morris said.

"I would," George Ross said.

Washington nodded his head in approval. "That is further proof to me that the separation is coming soon," he said. "I should like everything to be ready for it when it comes. I have an idea about this flag." He spoke with enthusiasm and his face glowed. "It would please me very much if you will meet me here tomorrow after the session of Congress ends. I think I shall have something to show you then."

11

The Flag Committee

WASHINGTON HAD BEEN RIGHT WHEN HE SAID
that separation from England was not far off.
There were many signs of this. One sign was that
for some months now, in all the Colonies, the British governors and their helpers had been leaving
to return to England. They were afraid to stay.
Another sign was that in the week just past, the

94

Congress had advised each colony to form a government of its own in place of the British one. It had also advised the Colonies to call themselves states. Certainly soon there would be a declaration of independence. And after that there would be a United States of America.

Washington knew what the Congress had done. Furthermore he could feel the things that were coming. He knew, also, that in a very few days he would have to leave Philadelphia to return to his army. Before he left he wanted to take care of as many matters as he could. One of the matters he wanted decided was that of the national flag.

On the afternoon after he had talked to Morris and George Ross, he did not have to attend the Congress. So he stayed at his hotel, writing orders to his colonels, checking dispatches he had received, and figuring again and again how to make the most of his limited military supplies.

But he had not forgotten his appointment or his decision of the day before. Every now and then he reached toward his pocket for his watch fob, a ribbon with dangling gold seals. He took out his thick gold watch and looked at it. Once or twice, because time seemed to be passing so slowly, he held the watch to his ear to be sure it was still running. Finally it was time for the meeting and he left the hotel.

His coach and coachman were waiting for him, and Washington asked to be driven to the State House. Just as the coach pulled up in front of the State House, he saw Ross and Morris. They were talking to some of the other delegates, but they excused themselves and came over to him.

"Well?" Robert Morris said, smiling up at the General. In that one rather gay, questioning word Morris said, *You asked us to be here. We are here. Now what about it?*

Morris's good nature and charm always had a warming effect on Washington, and this meeting was no exception. His many cares dropped away

96

from him temporarily, leaving him with only enthusiasm for the project he had in mind.

"Would you like to come into the coach with me?" Washington asked. "Or shall we go for a walk?"

"We might, perhaps, sit in the park," Morris suggested.

Washington nodded. He climbed down from the coach and, walking between the other two, led the way toward the mall.

When they were seated on a bench, Washington said, "I have had the three of us appointed as a committee."

"A committee?" George Ross said.

"Why?" Morris asked.

"It is unofficial, as yet," Washington told them. "But it is still a committee. That is better than nothing. As a committee we are to design a flag for all the Colonies. Or we are to approve a design. We are to have a flag made from the design we

97

choose. Then the flag will be ready when the moment is ripe."

"I am glad this has been done," Morris said. "It is high time."

"Again I marvel, General, that you find the opportunity to attend to everything," George Ross said. "But I, too, am glad it has been done."

George Washington put his hand slowly into his pocket. He drew out a folded piece of paper. He unfolded it and laid it in front of the other men.

"This is a design for a flag that has been drawn for me," he said. "I think it is good."

George Ross and Robert Morris examined the sketch. Part of the new flag was like the Grand Union flag. In the field there were thirteen alternating red and white stripes. But part of it was quite different, for in the blue canton there was a circle of thirteen six-pointed white stars. Together, canton and field made a flag which was entirely unlike any flag the Colonies had ever had before.

"This is good," Robert Morris said. "This is a flag that can be clearly distinguished at sea."

"And this is a flag that cannot be mistaken on land," George Ross said. "Furthermore, there is nothing left in it that is British."

"Yes, it is American." George Washington smiled with pleasure, then grew serious. "I hope it is also a flag that means standing together," he said. "It seems to me to show unity and strength. I should like very much to see it made up."

"I wonder," he said after a little, "if there is a flag-maker in the city."

"There is no official flag-maker that I know of," Morris said. "But could not some woman who sews well make a flag?"

George Ross took out his snuff-box and juggled it in his hand. "I know of one who could do it," he said. "She is in business as an upholsterer. She is an excellent seamstress and a hard worker. She is also the widow of my nephew, so I know her well. Her name is Betsy Ross."

"The widow?" Washington said slowly. "I have met your nephew. I did not know he had died."

"He was killed some six months ago," Ross said. "He was guarding military stores on the wharf here when there was an explosion. It is a very sad matter and his death is a great loss to us." He sighed. "I am sorry to say that I was one of the ones who had him stationed there."

"My committee is responsible for shipping in these supplies," Robert Morris said. "Perhaps if someone had been more careful, there would have been no explosion."

"Perhaps," George Ross said. "But one cannot look back nor measure these things. There are always some young men who die needlessly at times like these." He stood up. "I do not like to press the matter of the seamstress, sir, but I really believe my niece can cut and stitch together a flag if you want her to. She is experienced in all forms of sewing. And when she makes up her mind to do something, nothing can stop her."

Washington rose, too. He smiled at George Ross. "You are not pressing it," he said. "I also know Mistress Ross. And she is all you say she is. She has embroidered cuffs and ruffles for me sometimes. Perhaps I am wearing one now that was made by her. Let me see." He pulled down his shirt cuff and looked at it. He bent his head to examine the ruffle on his chest. "Yes, this is one of hers," he said. "See how fine it is. How perfect. We shall take her our sketch. She is the one to make our flag."

12

The Visit

IT WAS NOT AN EXTRAORDINARY THING FOR BETSY
Ross to hear a coach come rumbling over the cob-
blestones of Arch Street. It was not an unusual
thing for her to hear a coach stopping in front of

her door. But Betsy was curious enough to run to the front window and peep through the shutters whenever she heard such a sound. She wanted always to know who was visiting her and to try to guess what he might order from her shop.

On this early summer afternoon in 1776 she was on the second floor in her bedroom when she heard the sound. She was measuring the canopy and ruffles on her big four-poster bed, because she had an order to make some like it, and she wanted them to fit exactly. She was figuring out how much material she would need.

As she heard the coach stop, she jumped down from a low stepladder and ran to the window. She saw three men get out of the coach. One wore a gray suit, one wore a brown suit, and the tallest of the three had on a blue-and-buff uniform.

The tall man looked up, as if to make sure that this narrow brick house with the sharply sloping roof was the one he was seeking. Betsy saw the ruddy face, the blue-gray eyes, the long nose. She recognized General Washington. The man in the gray suit started toward her house and she recognized John's uncle. Robert Morris spoke to the coachman, and as he raised his head to do so, she recognized him, too.

It would not have surprised her to see any one of these men standing alone on her front walk. After all, she knew them and she knew they all needed things she could make. But it did surprise her to see them coming together toward her house. *They are so busy these days,* she thought, *they could surely not take time just to go shopping together. And the General is so much busier than any of them. Surely he can't have time for the nice things that everyone knows he loves.* Then for a minute she did not care why they were there. She was simply pleased that General Washington had arrived, once more, at her shop.

She heard a knock at the door. She dashed to the mirror to make sure her hair was tucked neatly within her cap. She straightened her skirt and her

apron and ran down the steep, narrow stairs to
open the front door.

Betsy and her visitors exchanged greetings and
then stood for a short time in the front parlor.
Washington was so tall that the small room
seemed to shrink around him.

George Ross said, "May we go into your back
parlor to talk, please? We can be just as comfortable there and no one will see or disturb us."

Most of the work of the shop was done in the
back parlor, which adjoined the front one. Betsy
could be glad now of her long-time habits of neat-
ness and cleanliness, because everything in the
back room was as ready for her visitors as if she
had known they were coming. The wide boards
of her floor were spotless, the white walls looked as
if they had been freshly painted. The brass and-
irons gleamed, the wood furniture had a beeswax
shine, the treasures in the corner cupboard were
dusted and ready for use. The materials for her
work were stored in the bottom part of this cup-

board and in the drawers of a chest that stood against one of the walls. The windows of the room were open and a fine fresh breeze blew in.

Betsy asked the men to be seated. They waited until she had found a chair, then they sat down. All three looked eager and interested.

"Will you tell Mistress Ross why we have come, please?" George Washington said to George Ross.

"We are a committee," George Ross began. And then he went on to tell her most of the things he and the others had discussed that day and the day before about a flag.

Betsy's first astonishment was that a committee should have spent some of its time talking about her. She had always kept so busy with her work or her friends or her family that she had not had time to think of herself as gaining a reputation for industry and skill.

She thanked her husband's uncle with a smile for the nice words he was repeating about her.

"We want the flag to be well made," George

Ross finished. "We want you to make the flag."

"Have you a picture of it?" Betsy asked.

George Washington reached into his pocket again for the sketch. He walked over to Betsy's desk, unfolded the paper and smoothed it out. He examined the drawing carefully, squinting his eyes to look at it.

Betsy came and stood beside him. Then the other two men crossed the bare wood floor and leaned over the desk also to examine the sketch once more.

After a long time Betsy said, "It is very nice. It should make a beautiful flag."

"You see what it means, don't you?" Washington said. "A circle of stars is union. Once the Colonies have joined, they will never disjoin."

"One star for each state," Robert Morris said, "and every star equal."

"Each equal part is needed to make up the whole," George Ross said.

It began to sound as if they were reciting a poem.

"Every part of the circle must be there to keep the whole circle perfect."

"A star is a symbol of light and truth."

"Blue is a strong color."

"White is a pure color."

"Red is a brave color."

Then suddenly they were all a little shy because they had said so much of what they were feeling. Robert Morris overcame his shyness by becoming practical. "Can you think of any way to improve the design?" he asked.

Betsy was almost afraid to make a suggestion, but since they all wanted the flag to be the best that it could be, and since she knew that she had a good idea, she spoke. "I think they should be five-pointed stars," she said. "They will look neater, cleaner and stronger that way."

"I agree that five-pointed stars would look better," Washington said. "But are they not harder to make?"

"Not when one is used to cutting," Betsy said, speaking with confidence now. "And once the star design is made, it will be an easy one to copy. I can make a five-pointed star."

The committee discussed this for a little, then decided that the five-pointed star would be an improvement. Soon they wanted Betsy's opinion on the proportions of the flag and materials for it. They sat down again and listened while she talked of the relation of length to width, and of fine buntings and dyes.

When she had finished George Ross said, "General, if you would care to have a new sketch made, I can bring it back here for you."

Washington made some notes on the sketch and put it back into his pocket. "Very well," he said. Then he rose to leave. "I envy you the making of the flag, Mistress Ross. It is always so much more delightful to be able to make things than to have to destroy them." He started walking from the back parlor toward the front. "That is why I feel so strongly about my plantation and growing things there and making improvements," he said. "That is why I wish so often that I could return there and resume my old life."

At the door he stopped, tall, dignified, courteous. "We have talked so much," he said, "and we have not asked you the one important question. Can you make a flag?"

Betsy looked up at him. Her blue eyes were steady and serious. "I never have," she said, "but I'll try."

13

Betsy Makes a Flag

THE MEN OF THE COMMITTEE HAD TOLD BETSY
that it would be better not to talk about the flag
for a while. They advised her to wait until it was
finished and then they would see how far the
Congress had gone toward declaring itself a union
of independent states. They were sure they would

know soon if the Congress wished to break away forever from England.

So Betsy told no one of the committee's visit.

Even after George Ross had returned with the new sketch, and after she and he had examined and discussed it and decided that it was an improvement, she still told no one. She merely told her customers that for a time she would be too busy to take on any new work. After that, for a few days, there was almost no one around the shop to bother her.

From the sketch she figured out how much material of each color she would need, and then she went out to buy it. She knew that bunting, because it is a sturdy, loosely woven cloth, would be the best material. Betsy could recognize good quality when she saw it and she examined the bunting carefully. She could also tell whether the dyes used were good or bad, for she herself had dyed much yarn at home, making red from cochineal and blue from indigo. She was very particular about the way the yarn in this bunting was dyed. When she was satisfied that she had found the best material for her purpose that Philadelphia had to offer, she started toward home.

On her way she decided that it was not enough merely to say one would try to do something. It was also necessary to learn *how* it could be done. For this purpose she walked into a store where supplies for ships were sold and asked to look at some flags. If the clerk there thought it strange that a woman should be doing this, he said nothing, but brought the flags to her.

She examined the binding, then the holes where the flag could be fastened to a rope and so to a flagstaff. She examined the way designs were sewn on. She examined the seams. Everything, of course, was sewn by hand. *Humph*, she thought, *I can certainly sew finer seams than that.*

She was so particular in her examination that the clerk became curious. "Are you going to make a flag for a company of the militia?" he asked.

Betsy lowered her eyes. "No," she said demurely.

"For a regiment?"

She did not think she should answer, but she could not resist it. She could not even resist a special little smile of pride. "It may be for something larger than a regiment," she said. Then she hurried out of the shop before the clerk could ask her any more questions.

When she was once more in her own house, she wondered how she could arrange the parts of the flag for sewing. She decided that the best way would be to set up her quilting frame in her back parlor and let the frame hold the strips of material steady while she stitched them together.

When she was ready to cut the bunting, her hand trembled. Usually Betsy cut boldly and quickly, sure of what she was doing. Now she hesitated. She measured and measured. Finally she plunged. She cut the seven red stripes and the six white ones. She cut the blue canton. Then

General Washington unfolded the sketch for the flag.

she took the paper pattern of a star which she had made so carefully and laid it on the white bunting. She cut around it thirteen times. She took the thirteen five-pointed white stars, covered them with an extra piece of cloth to keep them clean, and laid them away in a drawer of her chest. She would not need them until later on.

Betsy became so absorbed in what she was doing that it was long after her usual supper time when she remembered to go down to her basement kitchen to prepare the evening meal.

By the next afternoon the pieces in the quilting frame had begun to take on the look of a flag. Betsy was so busily at work that she did not hear a knock on her door. A step sounded in the front room, and when Betsy looked up she saw the Rector of her church walking through the front room and coming to a stop at the threshold of the back parlor. He was carrying a small bundle.

Betsy remembered then that she had promised to mend an altar cloth for him and had forgotten it in the rush of this new work. She apologized, and with a smile the Rector apologized for breaking in on her in such an unceremonious way.

Betsy knew there could be no harm in telling the Rector what she was doing, because she knew how closely he and Christ Church were tied to the patriot cause. She had been in the church when the entire Continental Congress had attended services. She had heard how, when the Continental Congress assembled in its own meeting place, the Rector had opened the first session with a prayer. Now she asked him to sit down, glad to have his intelligent, serene face across from her while she worked, glad to have his intelligent conversation to listen to and to have him to talk to.

She told him about the visit of the Committee and what they had asked her to do. She requested him not to speak of this yet to anyone else. After a while she got up, took the thirteen stars from the drawer and laid them on the blue bunting in the position they would have when she sewed them on. As she put each one down, smoothing it until it lay flat, she named the Colony it represented. "Pennsylvania," she said solemnly, like a chant, "New Hampshire, Rhode Island, Connecticut, New York, New Jersey, Massachusetts Bay, Delaware, Maryland, Virginia, North Carolina, South Carolina, Georgia. Thirteen states together." Then she sat at the frame again to sew once more.

"Shall I tell you a story?" the Rector asked.

Betsy had never outgrown her love of stories. There was nothing she liked better than to have somebody tell her a story or read one to her while she worked. "Yes," she said, "please do."

"This is a story about flags," the Rector said, "although it is more a history than a story. If you are going to be a flag-maker, you will, perhaps, want to know something about the history of flags."

Betsy nodded.

The Rector sat with his hands in his lap, pressing his finger tips together as he talked. "People of all times and of all countries have wanted emblems," he said. "They have wanted some sign to tell them they belonged together. Usually, in early times, they belonged together under a king or a tribal leader who was also their religious leader. Sometimes the king was so much the religious leader that they believed him to be their god. This was true, for instance, of the ancient Egyptians. Men in the Egyptian army carried standards or poles, and on these poles were symbols of their king, who was also their god. There would be a figure of an animal on top of this pole, or a tablet with the king's name inscribed on it, or a huge feather fan, or anything else which meant to them that they had sworn to be loyal to their king and to their god.

"It was a great honor to be the standard-bearer in those early days, just as it is an honor to be a colorbearer now.

"The Persians and the Assyrians and the ancient

Hebrews all had their staffs with emblems on them. Sometimes there were streamers like flags under the emblems. Sometimes the emblems were attached to the chariots of the leaders. The Persian and Egyptian ships had embroidered sails, which were, perhaps, their flags. I suppose it was just as necessary in those days as it is today to be able to tell to what country a ship belonged." He looked at Betsy. "Shall I go on?" he asked.

She nodded again.

"I like to think of the beginning days of the Roman republic," the Rector said. "There the first battle emblem was a handful of hay tied to a pole. And I like to think of the famous eagle of Rome. Later on, of course, the Roman cavalry had a real flag. It was made of a square piece of fringed cloth. They took a spear with a crossbar and hung the flag from that.

"All this time, even when the flags were not really religious symbols, there still was a religious feeling about them. Men would sacrifice for them and die for them. They would do anything so that the emblem would not be dishonored.

"This was true in the Middle Ages as well. Those flags were made of fine materials like silk and velvet. Many of the symbols represented the saints. The leaders would choose a particular saint as their own and then use that saint's cross or sign. Sometimes the leader would be a true follower of the saint he chose. Sometimes he would be not at all like that saint.

"It is very easy to have emotions about a flag," the Rector said. "But sometimes it is very dangerous, too. We must be so sure that the flag represents what we truly believe in. We do not want to be led astray by beautiful colors or shapes or by what the symbol used to mean. Take, for instance, those British symbols of Saint Andrew and Saint George; those are two saints I might be quite willing to follow. But I am not willing to follow the present King, who has adopted them for his own."

"What will you do if the American states decide to become independent of the King of England?" Betsy asked.

"I already know the first thing I shall do," the Rector said. "I shall take our prayer book and cross out the prayer for the King that is in it." He smiled. "Perhaps that is a childish way of expressing my feeling," he said. "But on the other hand, it is hypocritical to keep that prayer there when we do not mean it." He stood up, ready to leave.

Betsy ran her needle through the bunting for safekeeping, then she rose, too. "Thank you so much," she said. "I enjoyed your story."

"It is always a pleasure to visit here," the Rector said. "You have the kind of faith in God and belief in His principles of justice which are needed in our struggles today. But you are also wise enough to know that faith must be implemented."

"What do you mean by that?" Betsy asked.

The Rector took her hand. "You believe that faith and effort go together," he said. "You work for what you believe in. Our church will be very proud of you, Mistress Ross, when it learns what you are doing now."

She followed him to the door. "Good-by," she said.

"Good-by. God bless you and give you success with your flag."

PART THREE

14

Afternoon in Congress

THE STATE HOUSE HAD A NEW NAME NOW. IT HAD a new purpose, too. It was no longer the headquarters of the governing body of the Colony of Pennsylvania. It was no longer even the meeting place of a Continental Congress which was trying to decide if the Colonies should separate from England. The Congress still met in the same place, but the governing body assembled there now had pledged itself. The decision had been made. The momentous decision had been made in that building. The Declaration of Independence had been written, approved there, and read out to the people. The people had cheered. The Liberty Bell had rung. The State House now received delegates, not from thirteen British Colonies, but from thirteen American states. There was still a war for Independence to be won. There was still a bitter and a long struggle ahead. But everyone knew that the war and the struggle *were* for independence. The State House was now called Independence Hall.

There is probably no more beautiful building anywhere than Independence Hall. Its meaning has given it added beauty, but it is beautiful even without its meaning. It is only two stories high, but it is stately, noble, majestic. It is less than half a block long, but it is spacious, solid, graceful. It was built slowly and with pride and care. Its bricks, brought from England, are laid in the interesting Old English Bond pattern, one long and one narrow, one red and one black. Its white clock tower rises naturally, without heaviness. Its doorways are wide and easy.

Inside the building there are ample rooms with great high ceilings, burnished white paneling, and big, brilliant chandeliers. There is a patterned brick floor in the welcoming hallway, and there are floors of fine woods in the rooms. There is a good curve to the archways and pillars.

Not much furniture is in the building, but what is there fits it well. The chairs and desks are made for use and beauty. They are made to serve and to last.

On Saturday, June 14, 1777, a man sat writing at a mahogany desk in one of the largest of the rooms in Independence Hall. A little behind him and to his left were the desk and chair of John Hancock, the President of the Congress. To his right were the tall windows. Directly behind him was one of the twin fireplaces. In front of him were the delegates to the Congress who were talking, listening, voting and discussing.

The man at the mahogany desk was Charles Thomson, secretary of the Congress, and he was hard at work fulfilling his duties—listening to everything and writing it down. He dipped his quill pen into an inkwell, pressed the pen against the paper and wrote:

"Resolved that the Flag of the United States consist of. . . ." He looked at what he had written. Then he drew a line through "consist of" and wrote above it "be distinguished by." He read it back to himself, moving his lips as he did so. "Resolved that the Flag of the United States be distinguished by. . . ." This still did not seem to be right. It was not the way the resolution had been framed. At least he did not think so. He gripped his pen tighter and tried again. He crossed out "distinguished by." He read the beginning of the resolu-

Independence Hall

tion once more. "Resolved that the Flag of the United States be. . . ." He nodded his head, satisfied. Then he wrote on. Finally he read the whole paragraph back to himself. Yes, he thought, this is right. This is the way it should be.

Softly he read the paragraph aloud, but only loud enough for his own ears.

"Resolved that the Flag of the United States be 13 stripes alternate red and white, that the Union be 13 stars white in a blue field representing a new constellation."

What a beautiful word constellation is, he thought. A new constellation. A new group of fixed stars, brilliant and steady. A new constellation to make light for all its people and for other people. Looking down at the Congressional Journal, with only the page and his own writing in front of him, he could almost see the new stars of America.

He shook himself out of his fancy, straightened his shoulders and glanced around the room. He would have to pay more attention to what the Congress was doing or he would miss the next resolution.

It had been such a busy session today, with all the reports from the Marine Committee and the resolutions to pay some accounts dating back to April and June. Then there had been the resolution just before the one about the flag. Charles Thomson looked at what he had written on that: "Resolved that the marine committee be empowered to give just directions respecting the continental ships of war in the river Delaware as they think proper in case the enemy succeed in their attempts on the said river." And then, just while he was recording that, someone had remembered that the Flag Committee's resolution had never been written down.

Now the Congress was in full discussion about Captain John Roach, and in a moment Thomson would be writing that in the record, too. He wiped his quill on a small cloth and made ready. "The council of the state of Massachusetts bay having represented by letter to the president of Congress that capt John Roach sometime since appointed to command the continental ship of war the Ranger is a person of doubtful Character and ought not to be intrusted with such a command, therefore Resolved that captain Roach be suspended."

While they discussed whom they should appoint to fill this captain's place, the secretary sat idle, listening. Because the delegates faced him, they sometimes seemed to be staring right at him. Thomson did not like to be stared at, so he gazed up at the large beautiful crystal chandelier above his head. He thought idly that if they did not finish soon, it would be almost dark enough to have the candles in the chandelier lighted. Yet he knew how much the Congress had to do these days, rushing its preparations to meet the attack of the enemy, planning to have Washington ward off Lord Howe's approach, giving assistance wherever possible.

Then the resolution was worded and he wrote

again. "Resolved that Captain John Paul Jones be appointed to command the said ship Ranger." "Resolved that William Whipple esq. member of Congress and of the marine committee John K. Langdon esq. continental agent and the said Capt John Paul Jones be authorized to appoint the lieutenant and other commissioned & warrant officers necessary for the said ship."

The decision in favor of John Paul Jones seemed to please the Congress. Men spoke of his past record, of how much sea experience he had had for one so young, and of his dashing, devil-may-care fighting spirit.

The business of the day went faster after that, and soon the meeting was over. The delegates broke up into small groups and left the building.

On their way out, two of Charles Thomson's friends stopped to wait for him. They stood beside his desk as he closed his journal and put his pens away.

"So finally we have an official flag," one of them said.

The other, a stocky man wearing a plum-colored suit, said, "I suppose it was official before, even though it was not written down. But lately there has been more confusion than ever among the standards carried by our forces. No one dared declare just what the flag of the republic was."

"It was not a matter of daring, but of time," the first man said. "The Congress had to say what the flag would be and we have not had time to do it."

"And we have sometimes been so busy that we have delayed on much more vital matters than this."

"Members of the Congress had previously said what the flag would be," Thomson told them. "But it was not thought necessary to record the resolution. We did not ever have time to record any resolution on the Grand Union flag, either. After all, compared to the defeat on Long Island, compaired to the capture of General Lee and certainly compared to all the dreadful sufferings of our army last winter, a thing like a flag is of little importance."

"You are quite right," the man in the plum-colored suit said. "But on the other hand, some say that the Stars and Stripes were carried at the battle of Trenton and that it meant a lot to the soldiers."

"If the flag was there," Charles Thomson said, "I'm sure it meant a lot to Washington, too." He opened the drawer of the desk and put his Journal of the Congress in it. "Some day soon we must let all the citizens know about this flag resolution," he said. "We must publish it in the newspapers."

15

The Makeshift Flag

ALTHOUGH CHARLES THOMSON, SECRETARY OF
the Continental Congress, had said that the flag
resolution must be published soon, there was no
mention of it in any newspapers until July. Then

through the month of August it was written up several times. But none of these notices was official. Thomson's did not appear in the newspapers until September, nearly three months after he had recorded the resolution in the Journal of the Congress.

Meanwhile, one quick-moving, daring sea captain was going about establishing the flag in his own way. This was John Paul Jones, new commander of the *Ranger*. As soon as he took command, he ordered the Stars and Stripes hoisted on his ship. Thus the *Ranger* became the first American warship with a truly national ensign. Later John Paul Jones was sent to France to deliver the news of Burgoyne's surrender. In the French harbor he demanded and received a salute of guns from a French man-of-war, the first official salute of any foreign country to the new nation and its flag, the first official recognition that the thirteen states *were* a nation.

Between the time that John Paul Jones first

hoisted the Stars and Stripes on the *Ranger* and the time that the *Ranger* received its salute in France, another first flag was talked about all through the Colonies. The story spread far and wide before Burgoyne's surrender. And it was a good story to be spread at that time because so many of the land battles were going against the Americans and people were often disheartened.

Betsy Ross heard about it when she was in William Richards' store buying a supply of bunting for new flags.

"Someone is trying to take your business away from you, Ma'am," the clerk told her.

Surprised, she looked up from her inspection of the bunting. Then she saw that he was laughing. "Why do you say that?" she asked.

"Haven't you heard the story of Fort Schuyler?" he said. He could not wait to tell her.

Standing with her hands on the bunting, Betsy listened and nodded and smiled while he told the story.

"You know where Fort Schuyler is," the clerk began. "In New York. They used to call it Fort Stanwix."

"I remember when I was a child," Betsy said, "my father told me a story about a treaty with the Six Nations of Indians that had been made at Fort Stanwix."

"That's the place," the clerk said. "But as I say, they call it Schuyler now. Well, anyway, the fort was being defended by us when the British and a lot of Indians attacked it. Lots of those Indians sign up with the British, you know."

"Some of them have a right to," Betsy said. "They don't understand what we're fighting for and besides, we haven't treated them properly. Penn used to, but we don't."

"Maybe so," the clerk said. "Anyway this is what happened."

He went on with the story, then, and told her that at the time of the British and Indian attack, the fort had been under the command of Colonel

Captain Swartwout handed them his blue coat.

Peter Gansevoort, who had tried to defend it with
six hundred men. This was not nearly enough, nor
were there enough supplies to last out a long siege.
The situation was dangerous, and help was needed.

Then from Albany, by way of the Mohawk
River, new troops arrived. They were the men of
the 9th Massachusetts Regiment and they brought
with them ammunition and supplies.

"But they also brought a newspaper," the clerk
said.

"A newspaper! What for?" Betsy exclaimed.

"It was a paper that announced the Flag Resolution by Congress," the clerk said. "These people at
Fort Schuyler hadn't known before that there was
any American flag. As soon as they read about it
they wanted one like it, but the new troops hadn't
brought a flag with them."

Betsy could imagine the scene that he described
next. The men who were defending the fort and
the families who lived in the fort with them decided they must have one of the new national em-

blems. The entire place was ransacked for suitable materials. There was no bunting or any cloth to be had by the yard, so whatever was at hand must be made to do. Women searched through their possessions. Children scurried around to find things for their parents. But a soldier was the first to have a practical idea. "I have a white shirt," he said. "It could be used for the white." There were many soldiers with just such shirts, so soon the white was no problem.

Then a soldier's wife came forward. She stammered and blushed at having to say this in public. "I have a red petticoat," she said. "It is wide and long. It has yards and yards of material in it, plenty for a flag."

Everyone laughed and then everyone stopped laughing and thanked her.

Now the only difficulty left was what to do about the blue. A young army captain by the name of Abraham Swartwout was standing in a group that was discussing this lack of one color.

A soldier's wife happened to glance at him, then stared hard. After a minute she looked sidewise at one of her women friends and back at the Captain. The second woman looked, too. Soon all the women there and a few of the men were staring as hard as they could at Swartwout. The Captain felt the stares and grew terribly self-conscious. He began to look down at his clothes. What was the matter? Then he saw that he was wearing a fine blue coat of just the right shade. He hesitated. He liked that coat and a good coat was a very hard thing to get in those days.

Suddenly he hesitated no longer. "I suppose if I don't give it up, it will be requisitioned," he said with a laugh.

The others smiled and said, "Yes. We would take it away from you."

He drew off his coat and handed it to them.

The next time he saw his coat it was the field of the union and the soldier's-shirt stars were sewn onto it. A group of women had gotten together early in the morning to make the flag and had finished it by afternoon.

"They say the stars were not in a circle," the clerk told Betsy. "They were in lines that followed the pattern of the old Union Jack."

"Well," Betsy said, "the resolution did not say how the stars were to be placed. Stars in rows might look very well indeed."

While the women at Fort Schuyler had been sewing a flag, some soldiers had put up a flagstaff on the corner of the fort that projected nearest the enemy. Then the makeshift flag was raised on this staff.

The drummer beat the assembly and everyone in the fort gathered to look up at the new flag. The adjutant general read to the defenders the resolution of Congress which had described the insignia of the flag of the new republic. A cannon was leveled at the enemy camp and fired.

Later that day some enemy flags were captured and, as trophies of victory, were immediately

16

The Star Spangled Banner

IT IS ONLY A COINCIDENCE THAT THE FATHER OF
the man who wrote *The Star Spangled Banner* had
a name which began with John Ross. John Ross
Key, he was called, and he named his son Francis
Scott Key.

Betsy Ross did not know this fact about the name of the father. But she knew the son's name and the words of the son's song, for the words became popular as soon as they were written and they were sung in many places and by many people throughout America. The tune she had known before, as did most people. It had first been the tune of an English song, "Anacreon in Heaven." Then, during the Revolution, this same air had been used for a song called "Adams and Liberty." But it was not until it was sung as "The Star Spangled Banner" that it gave people the impulse to rise to their feet, to put the best they had into their voices and to let go with triumphant rejoicing.

By the time Francis Scott Key's words were written, Betsy Ross was sixty-two years old. She was still active, though, still hard at work. She lived into her eighties and stayed active. She was still interested in flags and in what happened to the American flag.

In the thirty-seven years between the first congressional Flag Resolution and the writing of Francis Scott Key's song, many difficult changes took place in the new nation. The Revolutionary War was won. Washington's soldiers, afraid of the future without a monarch, invited him to become king, but he refused them, saying: "If I am not deceived in the knowledge of myself, you could not have found a person to whom your schemes could be more disagreeable." The Constitution was debated, struggled over, finally written and ratified. Washington was made President and at his inauguration the crowd cheered and cried out, "Long live George Washington, President of the United States!" John Adams and Jefferson and Madison were Presidents. The War of 1812 began.

During this same time of changes in the nation, some changes took place in the Stars and Stripes. The changes were needed because new states were admitted into the Union. Vermont was added on March 4, 1791 and Kentucky on June 1, 1792.

So thirteen stars and thirteen stripes no longer could be thought of as meaning a union of *all* the states.

Congress passed a bill to remedy this flag situation and President Washington signed it. "That from and after the first day of May, One Thousand seven hundred and ninety-five, the flag of the United States be fifteen stripes, alternate red and white, and that the Union be fifteen stars, white in a blue field."

So the flag which Francis Scott Key watched with such anxiety and such hope, the flag about which he wrote "The Star Spangled Banner," had fifteen stripes and fifteen stars.

Francis Scott Key was a slender, erect man with dark blue eyes and a thin, sensitive face. He was a lawyer, but he was also a poet. However, he did not take his poems very seriously. He wrote because he felt like writing, and he did not expect anyone to admire or care especially for his poems.

It was because he was an excellent lawyer that he had a chance to be a poet during the bombardment of Fort McHenry.

The War of 1812 had been going on for two years and the British were again fighting the Americans. Our part in this contest had grown out of a war between Great Britain and France. The British, because of their problems with France, had felt they had to interfere with our shipping. We refused to let them do it and so were involved in the war.

A short time before the bombardment of Fort McHenry, the British had attacked and burned the city of Washington. There they had captured a well-known, well-liked American doctor by the name of William Beanes, and they were holding him prisoner on one of their warships.

Francis Scott Key, as a lawyer with a good practice in Washington, was asked to go to the British to see if he could arrange for the release of Dr. Beanes. Key took with him a Colonel Skinner who was the government agent for the exchange of prisoners; and they sailed down Chesapeake Bay from Baltimore to interview the Admiral of the British fleet. Nothing seemed at all out of the way as they came aboard the flagship, met the Admiral and talked to him about letting Dr. Beanes go.

The Admiral said of course Dr. Beanes could be released, why most certainly. Then the surprise came. The British were planning an unexpected attack on Baltimore and on Fort McHenry, which was the coast defense of that city. They were afraid that Key might have learned this secret and would let news of their preparations leak out. So they made him a kind of prisoner, too, telling him they would detain him until the attack was over. They put him on a small American ship, the *Minden*, and towed that ship to a mooring in Baltimore harbor. They set a guard of British marines over him.

Francis Scott Key knew that there was nothing he could do to stop the battle and, furthermore, that there was no way he could warn the Americans about it. He had no choice but to stand on the deck of the *Minden* and watch while the cannons from the British ships fired at the American shore.

The waiting and watching would have been difficult for anyone. For a man who felt things as deeply as Key did, it was a suspense as strong as pain. He paced the deck while the eyes of his guard stayed on him. He came back again and again to the side of the *Minden* and peered through the mists of evening, then through the black of night.

The battle, which had raged all day, went on throughout the night. Key could not tell who was winning or if the Americans could stand up under the bombardment. He only knew that the star-spangled flag had still been flying over Fort McHenry when night came on. It was impossible for him to try to sleep. All night long he continued to watch the shore, straining for a sight of the flag that would tell him the Americans were holding out. His suspense grew. His fears for the fort grew with it. Once in a while, as he tells in the song, a rocket or bomb would light the shore enough for him to see that "our flag was still there." But between times the dark would cover everything again.

Finally there was the first smoky light of dawn. He strained for another look. He saw the flag still fluttering over Fort McHenry. The peril to America was over.

His emotion was intense. It flowed into the triumphant and grateful words of his poem.

Later in the morning the British released him, and along with him they released his companion, Colonel Skinner, and the prisoner, Dr. Beanes. As they were taken toward shore, Francis Scott Key, with the tune of the old song beating in his mind, found an envelope in his pocket and scribbled down his poem. He was unable to go to sleep that night until he had rewritten and polished it. He could hardly wait for the next morning so that he could show it to a friend.

"It is very, very good," his friend said. "People will like it. They will understand it." He hummed the song in a low voice. "Blest with victory and peace, may the Heav'n-rescued land, praise the Power that hath made and preserved us a nation."

17

How Many Stars and Stripes?

THE UNITED STATES IS ONE OF THE YOUNGEST OF
the great nations in the world and it has one of the
oldest flags. Other countries far older than the
United States did not adopt their national emblems
until a much later period in their own history. The

present-day flag of Great Britain, for instance, was adopted in 1801, and that of France in 1794. Portugal decided what its flag would be in 1830, Italy in 1848, and Germany in 1871.

Yet even the American flag, with its long and honorable history, has not stayed exactly the same from 1777 until now. The reason for this is, of course, that the United States did not stay the same. It expanded gradually, as more and more states were added to the Union. Still, the general design and the idea and the meaning of the first Stars and Stripes have remained the same.

In other countries it has been possible to swear allegiance to a king or an emperor. Here, instead of the promise to follow royalty, there is allegiance to the flag, which is a symbol of the country itself and of each of its parts, the states.

When the country was made up of fifteen states, it had a fifteen-star, fifteen-stripe national standard. But long after this became unsuitable—because four more states had joined the Union—it was kept as the official flag. And it remained so for more than twenty years.

Then some members of Congress thought that the flag should again be re-designed. They had four states too many for the flag already, and it seemed probable that even more states would join. This time, however, they wanted a flag that would not have to be changed too much as the country changed. The representatives brought their ideas to the Congress, but they soon found there was much disagreement as to what a permanent flag should be.

So the Congress debated and debated. Did they have a right, they asked themselves, to change the emblem that told of our beginning as an independent nation? On the other hand, shouldn't the flag take into account all the states?

But if new stripes were to be added all the time, some other members of Congress argued, the flag would become too large or the stripes would have to become too narrow and the flag would be out of proportion or would lose its distinctness.

As for stars, still others said, a blue canton could always be arranged so as to appear clear and beautiful no matter how many stars were in it. Wasn't there some way they could keep it an easily distinguished, conspicuous flag which was like itself and only like itself? Wasn't there a way they could do this and still have it truly representative?

The Congress finally reasoned, in 1818, that there was a way to do all this. They could change the number of stars that represented the states. They could keep the stripes that represented the beginning of our history as a nation, that important period of the thirteen struggling states.

When the Congress at length ended its debating and voted, the decision was that the stripes would return to thirteen, and would always be thirteen. The decision on the stars was that there would be one for each state, and that "on the admission of every new state into the Union, one star be added to the union of the flag; and that such an addition should take effect on the fourth of July next succeeding such admission."

President Monroe signed this bill on the fourth of April, 1818, and it has been the flag law of the United States ever since.

A later Congress established the Flag Day of the United States as June fourteenth. This date commemorates the Flag Resolution first inscribed at the Continental Congress.

People have many different ideas as to what flag etiquette should be. Throughout the years individuals handled the flag in one way, organizations in another, military men in a third. Some people insisted that customs were laws, others that laws were only customs. So in 1942 the Congress passed a "joint resolution to codify and emphasize existing rules and customs pertaining to the display and use of the flag of the United States of America." Six months later it was felt that this law was a little too military and that regulations for civilians and civilian groups should be added to the law.

These are the civilian regulations for flag etiquette which the Congress established:

SEC. 2. (*a*) It is the universal custom to display the flag only from sunrise to sunset on buildings and on stationary flagstaffs in the open. However, the flag may be displayed at night upon special occasions when it is desired to produce a patriotic effect.

(*b*) The flag should be hoisted briskly and lowered ceremoniously.

(*c*) The flag should not be displayed on days when the weather is inclement.

(*d*) The flag should be displayed on all days when the weather permits, especially on New Year's Day, January 1; Inauguration Day, January 20; Lincoln's Birthday, February 12; Washington's Birthday, February 22; Army Day, April 6; Easter Sunday (variable); Mother's Day, second Sunday in May; Memorial Day (half-staff until noon), May 30; Flag Day, June 14; Independence Day, July 4; Labor Day, first Monday in September; Constitution Day, September 17; Columbus Day, October 12; Navy Day, October 27; Armistice Day, November 11; Thanksgiving Day, fourth Thursday in November; Christmas Day, December 25; such other days as may be proclaimed by the President of the United States; the birthdays of States (dates of admission); and on State holidays.

(*e*) The flag should be displayed daily, weather permitting, on or near the main administration building of every public institution.

(*f*) The flag should be displayed in or near every polling place on election days.

(*g*) The flag should be displayed during school days in or near every schoolhouse.

SEC. 3. That the flag, when carried in a procession with another flag or flags, should be either on the marching right; that is, the flag's own right, or, if there is a line of other flags, in front of the center of that line.

(*a*) The flag should not be displayed on a float in a parade except from a staff, or as provided in subsection (*i*).

(*b*) The flag should not be draped over the hood, top, sides, or back of a vehicle or of a railroad train or a boat. When the flag is displayed on a motorcar, the staff shall be fixed firmly to the chassis or clamped to the radiator cap.

(*c*) No other flag or pennant should be placed above or, if on the same level, to the right of the flag of the United States of America, except during church services conducted by naval chaplains at sea, when the church pennant may be flown above the flag during church services for the personnel of the Navy.

(*d*) The flag of the United States of America, when it is displayed with another flag against a wall from crossed staffs, should be on the right, the flag's own right, and its staff should be in front of the staff of the other flag.

(*e*) The flag of the United States of America should be at the center and at the highest point of the group when a number of flags of States or localities or pennants of societies are grouped and displayed from staffs.

(*f*) When flags of States, cities, or localities, or pennants of societies are flown on the same halyard with the flag of the United States, the latter should always be at the peak. When the flags are flown from adjacent staffs, the flag of the United States should be hoisted first and lowered last. No such flag or pennant may be placed above the flag of the United States or to the right of the flag of the United States.

(*g*) When flags of two or more nations are displayed, they are to be flown from separate staffs of the same height. The flags should be of approximately equal size. International usage forbids the display of the flag of one nation above that of another nation in time of peace.

(*h*) When the flag of the United States is displayed from a staff projecting horizontally or at an angle from the window sill, balcony, or front of a building, the union of the flag should be placed at the peak of the staff unless the flag is at half-staff. When the flag is suspended over a sidewalk from a rope extending from a house to a pole at the edge of the sidewalk, the flag should be hoisted out, union first, from the building.

(*i*) When the flag is displayed otherwise than by being flown from a staff, it should be displayed flat, whether indoors or out, or so suspended that its folds fall as free as though the flag were staffed.

(*j*) When the flag is displayed over the middle of the street, it should be suspended vertically with the union to the north in an east and west street or to the east in a north and south street.

(*k*) When used on a speaker's platform, the flag, if displayed flat, should be displayed above and behind the speaker. When displayed from a staff in a church or public auditorium, if it is displayed in the chancel of a church, or on the speaker's platform in a public auditorium, the flag should occupy the position of honor and be placed at the clergyman's or speaker's right as he faces the congregation or audience. Any other flag so displayed in the chancel or on the platform should be placed at the clergyman's or speaker's left as he faces the congregation or audience. But when the flag is displayed from a staff in a church or public auditorium elsewhere than in the chancel or on the platform it shall be placed in the position of honor at the right of the congregation or audience as they face the chancel or platform. Any other flag so displayed should be placed on the left of the congregation or audience as they face the chancel or platform.

(*l*) The flag should form a distinctive feature of the ceremony of unveiling a statue or monument, but it should never be used as the covering for the statue or monument.

(*m*) The flag, when flown at half-staff, should be first hoisted to the peak for an instant and then lowered to the half-staff position. The flag should be again raised to the peak before it is lowered for the day. By "half-staff" is meant lowering the flag to one-half the distance between the top and bottom of the staff. Crepe streamers may be affixed to spearheads or flagstaffs in a parade only by order of the President of the United States.

(*n*) When the flag is used to cover a casket, it should be so placed that the union is at the head and over the left shoulder. The flag should not be lowered into the grave or allowed to touch the ground.

SEC. 4. That no disrespect should be shown to the flag of the United States of America, the flag should not be dipped to any person or thing. Regimental colors, State flags, and organization or institutional flags are to be dipped as a mark of honor.

(*a*) The flag should never be displayed with the union down save as a signal of dire distress.

(*b*) The flag should never touch anything beneath it, such as the ground, the floor, water, or merchandise.

(*c*) The flag should never be carried flat or horizontally, but always aloft and free.

(*d*) The flag should never be used as drapery of any sort whatsoever, never festooned, drawn back, nor up, in folds, but always allowed to fall free. Bunting of blue, white, and red, always arranged with the blue above, the white in the middle, and the red below, should be used for covering a speaker's desk, draping the front of a platform, and for decoration in general.

(*e*) The flag should never be fastened, displayed, used, or stored in such a manner as will permit it to be easily torn, soiled, or damaged in any way.

(*f*) The flag should never be used as a covering for a ceiling.

(*g*) The flag should never have placed upon it, nor on any

part of it, nor attached to it any mark, insignia, letter, word, figure, design, picture, or drawing of any nature.

(*h*) The flag should never be used as a receptacle for receiving, holding, carrying, or delivering anything.

(*i*) The flag should never be used for advertising purposes in any manner whatsoever. It should not be embroidered on such articles as cushions or handkerchiefs and the like, printed or otherwise impressed on paper napkins or boxes or anything that is designed for temporary use and discard; or used as any portion of a costume or athletic uniform. Advertising signs should not be fastened to a staff or halyard from which the flag is flown.

(*j*) The flag, when it is in such condition that it is no longer a fitting emblem for display, should be destroyed in a dignified way, preferably by burning.

SEC. 5. That during the ceremony of hoisting or lowering the flag or when the flag is passing in a parade or in a review, all persons present should face the flag, stand at attention, and salute. Those present in uniform should render the military salute. When not in uniform, men should remove the headdress with the right hand holding it at the left shoulder, the hand being over the heart. Men without hats should salute in the same manner. Aliens should stand at attention. Women should salute by placing the right hand over the heart. The salute to the flag in the moving column should be rendered at the moment the flag passes.

SEC. 6. That when the national anthem is played and the flag is not displayed, all present should stand and face toward the music. Those in uniform should salute at the first note of the anthem, retaining this position until the last note. All others should stand at attention, men removing the headdress. When the flag is displayed, all present should face the flag and salute.

SEC. 7. That the pledge of allegiance to the flag, "I pledge allegiance to the flag of the United States of America and to the Republic for which it stands, one Nation indivisible, with liberty and justice for all," be rendered by standing with the right hand over the heart. However, civilians will always show full respect to the flag when the pledge is given by merely standing at attention, men removing the headdress. Persons in uniform shall render the military salute.

Sec. 8. Any rule or custom pertaining to the display of the flag of the United States of America, set forth herein, may be altered, modified, or repealed, or additional rules with respect thereto may be prescribed, by the Commander-in-Chief of the Army and Navy of the United States, whenever he deems it to be appropriate or desirable; and any such alteration or additional rule shall be set forth in a proclamation.

The United States Marine Corps, in its booklet entitled *How to Respect and Display Our Flag,* shows how much of each day the flag is aloft somewhere around the globe. It states:

"It is the custom of the U. S. Marines to raise the Flag every morning at 8:00 o'clock. It remains flying until sunset. Three hours after the Marines at Parris Island, S. C., and other east coast naval stations have raised the Flag, other Marines at San Diego, Calif., or other posts along the Pacific seaboard present arms to the colors as they are hauled smartly to the top of the flagstaff. About two and a half hours after the National Standard is raised at San Diego, the ceremony is repeated in the Hawaiian Islands. Several hours afterward, the western march of daylight catches the fluttering folds of the Stars and Stripes flying over American Consulates in the Near East or Great Britain, and when the sun has passed its zenith in the Old World, the Flag is again flung to the breeze on the Atlantic seaboard. Thus the Stars and Stripes makes its appearance in the early morning and remains flying until the sun disappears over the horizon—a symbol of justice for those who sought liberty under its folds."

When It Happened

1752   Jan. 1. Betsy Griscom born.

1765   The Stamp Act.

1766   Repeal of the Stamp Act.

1773   Nov. 4. Betsy Griscom married to John Ross.

1773   Dec. 16. The Boston Tea Party.

1774   Sept. 5. First Continental Congress (held in Carpenter's Hall).

1775   Apr. 18. Battles of Lexington and Concord.

1775   May 10. Second Continental Congress (held in State House).

1775   June 15. Washington made commander-in-chief of Continental Army.

1775   June 17. Battle of Bunker Hill.

1775   July 1. Washington took command of troops at Cambridge.

1776   Jan. 2. Grand Union Flag unfurled at Cambridge.

1776   Jan. Grand Union Flag raised on the *Alfred*.

1776   Jan. 21. John Ross buried.

1776   May 23 to June 7. Washington in Philadelphia.

1776   July 4. Declaration of Independence (made at State House, now called Independence Hall).

1776   Dec. 26. Battle of Trenton.

1777   May 29. Order for payment 14 pounds, 12 shillings, 2 pence by Pennsylvania State Navy Board to Elizabeth Ross for making ship's colors.

1777   June 14. Stars and Stripes resolution adopted by Congress.

1777   July 4. Stars and Stripes hoisted on the *Ranger* on orders from John Paul Jones.

1777   Aug. 3. The improvised Stars and Stripes raised at Fort Schuyler.

1777   July through Aug. Stars and Stripes mentioned in newspapers.

1777   Sept. 2 & 3. Stars and Stripes resolution of Congress officially published in Philadelphia and other newspapers.

1777   Feb. 14. The *Ranger* saluted by a French man-of-war.

1814   Sept. 13. The Star Spangled Banner written.

LANDMARK BOOKS

The Voyages of Christopher Columbus by Armstrong Sperry

The Landing of the Pilgrims by James Daugherty

Pocahontas and Captain John Smith by Marie Lawson

Paul Revere and the Minute Men by Dorothy Canfield Fisher

Our Independence and the Constitution by Dorothy Canfield Fisher

The California Gold Rush by May McNeer

The Pony Express by Samuel Hopkins Adams

Lee and Grant at Appomattox by MacKinlay Kantor

The Building of the First Transcontinental Railroad by Adele Nathan

The Wright Brothers by Quentin Reynolds

Prehistoric America by Anne Terry White

The Vikings by Elizabeth Janeway

The Santa Fe Trail by Samuel Hopkins Adams

The Story of the U. S. Marines by George Hunt

The Lewis and Clark Expedition by Richard L. Neuberger

The Monitor and the Merrimac by Fletcher Pratt

The Explorations of Père Marquette by Jim Kjelgaard

The Panama Canal by Bob Considine

The Pirate Lafitte and the Battle of New Orleans by Robert Tallant

Custer's Last Stand by Quentin Reynolds

Daniel Boone by John Mason Brown

Clipper Ship Days by John Jennings

Gettysburg by MacKinlay Kantor

The Louisiana Purchase by Robert Tallant

Wild Bill Hickok Tames the West by Stewart H. Holbrook

Betsy Ross and the Flag by Jane Mayer

The Conquest of the North and South Poles by Russell Owen

Ben Franklin of Old Philadelphia by Margaret Cousins

Trappers and Traders of the Far West by James Daugherty

Mr. Bell Invents the Telephone by Katherine Shippen

The Barbary Pirates by C. S. Forester

Sam Houston, The Tallest Texan by William Johnson

The Winter at Valley Forge by Van Wyck Mason

The Erie Canal by Samuel Hopkins Adams

Thirty Seconds Over Tokyo by Ted Lawson and Bob Considine

Thomas Jefferson by Vincent Sheean

37 **The Coming of the Mormons** by Jim Kjelgaard

38 **George Washington Carver** by Anne Terry White

39 **John Paul Jones** by Armstrong Sperry

40 **The First Overland Mail** by Robert Pinkerton

41 **Teddy Roosevelt and the Rough Riders** by Henry Castor

42 **To California by Covered Wagon** by George R. Stewart

43 **Peter Stuyvesant of Old New York** by Anna and Russel Crouse

44 **Lincoln and Douglas** by Regina Z. Kelly

45 **Robert Fulton and the Steamboat** by Ralph Nading Hill

46 **The F.B.I.** by Quentin Reynolds

47 **Dolly Madison** by Jane Mayer

48 **John James Audubon** by Margaret and John Kieran

49 **Hawaii** by Oscar Lewis

50 **War Chief of the Seminoles** by May McNeer

51 **Old Ironsides, The Fighting Constitution** by Harry Hansen

52 **The Mississippi Bubble** by Thomas B. Costain

53 **Kit Carson and the Wild Frontier** by Ralph Moody

54 **Robert E. Lee and the Road of Honor** by Hodding Carter

55 **Guadalcanal Diary** by Richard Tregaskis

56 **Commodore Perry and the Opening of Japan** by Ferdinand Kuhn

57 **Davy Crockett** by Stewart H. Holbrook

58 **Clara Barton, Founder of the American Red Cross** by Helen Dore Boylston

59 **The Story of San Francisco** by Charlotte Jackson

60 **Up the Trail from Texas** by J. Frank Dobie

61 **Abe Lincoln: Log Cabin to White House** by Sterling North

62 **The Story of D-Day: June 6, 1944** by Bruce Bliven, Jr.

63 **Rogers' Rangers and the French and Indian War** by Bradford Smith

64 **The World's Greatest Showman: The Life of P. T. Barnum** by J. Bryan II

65 **Sequoyah: Leader of the Cherokees** by Alice Marriott

66 **Ethan Allen and the Green Mountain Boys** by Slater Brown

67 **Wyatt Earp: U. S. Marshal** by Stewart H. Holbrook

68 **The Early Days of Automobiles** by Elizabeth Janeway

69 **The Witchcraft of Salem Village** by Shirley Jackson

70 **The West Point Story** by Colonel Red Reeder & Nardi Reeder Campion

LANDMARK BOOKS *continued*

71 **George Washington: Frontier Colonel**
by Sterling North

72 **The Texas Rangers**
by Will Henry

73 **Buffalo Bill's Great Wild West Show**
by Walter Havighurst

74 **Evangeline and the Acadians**
by Robert Tallant

75 **The Story of the Secret Service**
by Ferdinand Kuhn

76 **Tippecanoe and Tyler, Too!**
by Stanley Young

77 **America's First World War**
by Henry Castor

78 **The Doctors Who Conquered Yellow Fever** by Ralph Nading Hill

WORLD LANDMARK BOOKS

W-1 **The First Men in the World**
by Anne Terry White

W-2 **Alexander the Great** by John Gunther

W-3 **Adventures and Discoveries of Marco Polo** by Richard J. Walsh

W-4 **Joan of Arc** by Nancy Wilson Ross

W-5 **King Arthur and His Knights**
by Mabel L. Robinson

W-6 **Mary, Queen of Scots** by Emily Hahn

W-7 **Napoleon and the Battle of Waterloo** by Frances Winwar

W-8 **Royal Canadian Mounted Police**
by Richard L. Neuberger

W-9 **The Man Who Changed China**
by Pearl S. Buck

W-10 **The Battle of Britain**
by Quentin Reynolds

W-11 **The Crusades** by Anthony West

W-12 **Genghis Khan and the Mongol Horde** by Harold Lamb

W-13 **Queen Elizabeth and the Spanish Armada** by Frances Winwar

W-14 **Simón Bolívar** by Arnold Whitridge

W-15 **The Slave Who Freed Haiti**
by Katharine Scherman

W-16 **The Story of Scotland Yard**
by Laurence Thompson

W-17 **The Life of Saint Patrick**
by Quentin Reynolds

W-18 **The Exploits of Xenophon**
by Geoffrey Household

W-19 **Captain Cook Explores the South Seas** by Armstrong Sperry

W-20 **Marie Antoinette** by Bernardine Kielty

W-21 **Will Shakespeare and the Globe Theater** by Anne Terry White

W-22 **The French Foreign Legion**
by Wyatt Blassingame

W-23 **Martin Luther** by Harry Emerson Fosdick

W-24 **The Hudson's Bay Company**
by Richard Morenus

W-25 **Balboa: Swordsman and Conquistador** by Felix Riesenberg,

W-26 **The Magna Charta** by James Daugherty

W-27 **Leonardo da Vinci** by Emily Hahn

W-28 **General Brock and Niagara Falls**
by Samuel Hopkins Adams

W-29 **Catherine the Great**
by Katharine Scherman

W-30 **The Fall of Constantinople**
by Bernardine Kielty

W-31 **Ferdinand Magellan**
by Seymour Gates Pond

W-32 **Garibaldi: Father of Modern Italy**
by Marcia Davenport

W-33 **The Story of Albert Schweitzer**
by Anita Daniel